Brand and Myth

Stefan Waller

Brand and Myth

Stefan Waller
Zhejiang Wanli University
Ningbo, China

ISBN 978-3-662-70677-0   ISBN 978-3-662-70678-7 (eBook)
https://doi.org/10.1007/978-3-662-70678-7

© The Editor(s) (if applicable) and The Author(s), under exclusive license to Springer-Verlag GmbH, DE, part of Springer Nature 2025

Translation from the German language edition: "Marke und Mythos" by Stefan Waller, © Der/die Herausgeber bzw. der/die Autor(en), exklusiv lizenziert an Springer-Verlag GmbH, DE, ein Teil von Springer Nature 2024. Published by Springer Berlin Heidelberg. All Rights Reserved.

This book is a translation of the original German edition "Marke und Mythos" by Stefan Waller, published by Springer-Verlag GmbH, DE in 2024. The translation was done with the help of an artificial intelligence machine translation tool. A subsequent human revision was done primarily in terms of content, so that the book will read stylistically differently from a conventional translation. Springer Nature works continuously to further the development of tools for the production of books and on the related technologies to support the authors.

This work is subject to copyright. All rights are solely and exclusively licensed by the Publisher, whether the whole or part of the material is concerned, specifically the rights of translation, reprinting, reuse of illustrations, recitation, broadcasting, reproduction on microfilms or in any other physical way, and transmission or information storage and retrieval, electronic adaptation, computer software, or by similar or dissimilar methodology now known or hereafter developed.
The use of general descriptive names, registered names, trademarks, service marks, etc. in this publication does not imply, even in the absence of a specific statement, that such names are exempt from the relevant protective laws and regulations and therefore free for general use.
The publisher, the authors and the editors are safe to assume that the advice and information in this book are believed to be true and accurate at the date of publication. Neither the publisher nor the authors or the editors give a warranty, expressed or implied, with respect to the material contained herein or for any errors or omissions that may have been made. The publisher remains neutral with regard to jurisdictional claims in published maps and institutional affiliations.

This Springer imprint is published by the registered company Springer-Verlag GmbH, DE, part of Springer Nature.
The registered company address is: Heidelberger Platz 3, 14197 Berlin, Germany

If disposing of this product, please recycle the paper.

For Ben-Ming and Zhang Meng
My special thanks go to Hergen Hillen for his excellent editing, Ann-Kristin Iwersen and Justus Krüger for their careful reading and insightful suggestions, Oliver Errichiello for his professional support, and the Brand University of Applied Sciences and Zhejiang Wanli University for the opportunities offered to me at the Joint Institute of Zhejiang Wanli University and Brand University of Applied Sciences in Ningbo.

Foreword

> *... from a certain point in time, one no longer reads articles... only advertisements... they tell you everything...*
>
> Louis-Ferdinand Céline

Writings on issues of brands and brand advertising can usually be differentiated into two categories: On the one hand, committed polemics that denounce the insidious game of manipulating the "consumer" behavior, driven by algorithms that are no longer secret. On the other hand—in almost inexhaustible variety—scientific analyses, tools, and application templates that explain the nature of the buyer to brand managers at all hierarchical levels and markets, and provide practical tools for effectiveness control.

The brand and its communication lead a peculiar existence: it was and is always and everywhere (even in political systems that diametrically oppose the brand as a capitalist pillar of sanctity) and it is at the same time the curse of an enlightened consumer who, in view of ecological challenges, should buy rationally and not driven by affect. At the same time, it is a blessing, because it is, with regard to the everyday life of a post-postmodern era, the tool to realize the ideal of a self-determined and autonomous human existence. But how does the desire for uniqueness claim space?

The saying, "The more brands, the more individual the self," comes from the widely known everyday philosopher (and fashion designer) Wolfgang Joop. In this sense, the brand is the ideal tool to come as close as possible to the zeitgeist desires of a successful and fulfilled life. Through, with, and by the brand, people have the opportunity to realize their vision of a distinctive and special life. Because the brand marks its function as a "collectively anchored content storage" far beyond its performance function. The brand is used, utilized, and requested to enrich the individual with aspects and facets, perhaps even to equip them in the first place, which are beyond their creative possibilities and can be integrated in an uncomplicated way through a universal transaction medium, money. With this property, the brand performs a fascinating miracle structure: It is an object that enables a high claim to individuality, but it is only understood and can successfully realize its function if its message and signals are deeply standardized. A Rolex only makes sense if it is generally clear what owning a Rolex implies. The miracle of the brand is that it is "individual and standardized" at the same time.

If life is limited to our earthly presence, then it is precisely this life that we should experience in all its fullness and diversity. A crucial means to this end is the brand. Because in the best case, it has managed to stand for certain characteristics and even radiate them in such a way that they allow communicative connectivity independent of language and origin, transculturally and transhistorically: Brands are understood everywhere and they have always been part of social reality as forms of "compressed trust".

The essays compiled in this book do not follow the two categories of outrage or application previously outlined in their approach and perspective, but rather add a differently situated facet to the understanding of a vast phenomenon of global social reality: The revelation of deeply effective psychological and sociological dynamics that cannot be captured by either a politicized or an economic approach. In an atmosphere of "intellectual cheerfulness," it is possible to highlight the causal driving and enforcement forces of the brand in general and its variations and aesthetics in particular. Because, unlike the learned objects of scientifically based interpretation in art and media, the objects of everyday advertising communication are hardly ever the subject of deeper consideration and analysis. They are there to trigger an economic effect and must be abolished as quickly as possible so as not to appear as the cause of supposedly individual decisions. Nothing may be more disturbing for the people of our time than the suspicion that their actions are not their actions …

The advertising of the brand is and remains mostly in the infinity of reality without interpretation. But only a close examination allows an understanding of why the brand cannot be killed off either by political programming or by countless appeals to reason towards brand-fetishizing family members. On the contrary: The human turn towards the present will further fuel and strengthen the importance of the brand and its communication. The following considerations reveal this in a fascinating and surprising way.

This book is valuable: It is an attempt to look at an important, because original, level of understanding of being human in the age of acceleration (Hartmut Rosa). A level whose mass-effective manifestations appear and disappear so quickly that we do not become aware of the individual spotlights and their "inner implications". However: In their generalizing cuts and contents as well as their often tested aestheticizations for resonance and connectivity, they trace the desires, hopes, goals, fears, and realities of people in a changing world. The analyses of brands and their communication presented here attempt—with reference to science—to questioningly trace the realities. They hold back both an ethical and an economic judgment and instead create multifaceted thought images that impose questions. By making the question, not the answer, determine the view, this book is a rare philosophical confrontation with what actually concerns and determines the world, outside of academia. The view moves on the demanding ridge between search and knowledge. The level of psychology and sociology is also broken through and a philosophical level is drawn in. Therefore, the essays on the consumer realities of modernity extend far beyond the learned spheres of brand essence and into the question: What does it mean to live and experience in our time?

The chosen brands and examples thus become ciphers for general dynamics of both communal and societal developments. Especially in the German-speaking world, we often lack the ease of dealing with a scientifically grounded, literarily sophisticated, yet life-related observation—without a binary objective of knowledge.

This special, questioning, well-founded, and repeatedly amusing book has its purpose in itself: In the search for reality in the real … and that without advertising.

Hamburg   Oliver Errichiello
im January 2024

Brand and Myth—Relief in the Modern World

> "…it is wise to regard brands as sentient beings"
>
> Hans Domizlaff

In brands, the desires of modern humans emerge. In Nike, the hope of making it if you just do it; in a Mercedes, the pursuit of status, and in a MasterCard, the longing for those moments that money can't buy (but for which you still need some) is condensed. The list can be extended for a long time. Despite these brand messages being understood in various cultures, they lead a shadowy existence in the cultural philosophical debate. To professional thinkers, brands appear at best as banal and at worst as an instrument in a malignant context of deception. As an expression of capitalism, to which they are critical, and that usually means rejecting. In a more neutral attitude, dealing with brands is understood as a subject of business administration, marketing, and design, and thus located outside of their own competence.

Brands are particularly suitable as mirrors for understanding our existence in culture because they are consciously designed to resemble human individuality. This assumption is a remarkable central aspect of many considerations, mostly in the context of marketing, about the problem of branding. Here, most authors agree that we can treat brands as if they were people with individual personalities (see Burmann et al., 2012, p. 54 ff., Fioroni & Titterton, 2009, p. 29 ff; Qyll, 2021, p. 38 ff.). For *David A. Aaker*, it is also necessary for understanding our relationship with brands that we structurally understand them in accordance with human personality:

"To understand the nature of a brand-customer relationship, it is useful to consider the metaphor of a brand as a person who has personality and interpersonal relationship with customers." (Aaker, 1996, p. 51).

Raymond A. Nadeau describes "Living Brands" as "highly emotionalized personalities" (Nadeau, 2007, p. 4). *Azoulay and Kapferer* ultimately emphasize that the distinct human aspects are crucial for the description of brand personalities:

"It is time to restrict the use of the concept of brand personality to the meaning it should never have lost: 'the unique set of human personality traits both applicable and relevant to brands'." (Azoulay & Kapferer, 2003, p. 153).

These and many other authors take the possibility of an emotional relationship with the brand personality as a given. It is used as a basis for their own theory formation for the construction and management of brands, but is considered not to be in need of further explanation in itself. For example, in *Burmann et al.*, there is a reference to the perspective of animism, which we will discuss later, as a reason for the perception of brands as personalities. However, no further explanations are given about the animistic basis of the emotional bond between people and the object perceived as animated:

"Originally only related to humans, the theory of personality can also be transferred to brands or brand personalities (…) When designing the brand identity, the desired personality of the brand must therefore also be defined." (Burmann et al., 2012, p. 54).

As fitting as the approaches of these authors may be for further describing brand identity, it is still worthwhile to take a closer look at why we can perceive entities like brands as "personalities" at all. However, for this we need to dig a little deeper and initially move away from the focus on brands. For this endeavor, it is appropriate to rely on classic philosophical approaches that have been dealing with the world relationship arising from subjective human perceptual possibilities since at least *Immanuel Kant*. Kant emphatically points out that what the world is for us is significantly shaped by our own sensory experience and the categorical abilities of our mind:

"What the state of affairs with objects in themselves and apart from all this receptivity of our sensibility may be, remains completely unknown to us." (Kant 1790/1990, B 59/A 42).

Indeed, this is an assumption based on anthropological grounds, just as the function of transcendental categories can be observed as both gateways and blinders in relation to possible types of experiencing and recognizing in all living beings. Starting with the investigations of *Jakob von Uexküll* in the early twentieth century, biosemiotics deals with the fact that an animal can only recognize information as real if it is capable of interpreting it in its own way as "something", which also means ignoring all other perspectives on the world (cf. von Uexküll 1921). Following this, the human consciousness only experiences and recognizes those empirical data that our senses can perceive and that our mind can process. Conversely, things exist for us only in the way that we can deal with them with our physical and mental abilities. In Kant's terminology, this means that we cannot recognize things as they are outside of our own perspective—the respective "thing in itself". Everything that exists for us is shaped by the transcendental abilities of our mind, as conditions of the possibility of our sensory experience.

Following the Kantian tradition, the question of brand personality can thus be reformulated into the transcendental form: "What property of the human mind is the condition for the possibility of perceiving brands as personalities?" To ask this question means precisely not to search for specific forms, colors, sounds, prices, names, or advertising methods that emotionally appeal to us in relation to certain brands. The transcendental investigation rather means to make a change of perspective and to focus on the intellectual modes of our perception as the basis of this empirical experience. In relation to the question of branding, we therefore need to look closely at what contributes in our basic configuration as humans to experiencing brands as personalities.

In a first step, it is recommended to examine the difference between the perception of things and people more closely. We can initially ask ourselves the simple question of what exactly the difference is that qualifies something as a "thing" or as a "person". The most obvious answer highlights empirical findings that relate to all phenomena that we perceive when encountering other people: For example, other people are shaped in the broadest sense as we are; they move, feel, and smell like us and speak in a way that resembles the language we use ourselves. Although these empirical data are necessary for identifying persons as "persons", we must admit that these descriptions ultimately remain inadequate. For instance, we can imagine human beings for whom one or more of these descriptions do not fit. Moreover, we can now easily imagine machines that exhibit all possible externally human characteristics, including the ability to speak, but we still find it very difficult to refer to them as real persons.

Although it seems somewhat difficult or even impossible for us to name a single observable characteristic that distinguishes all beings endowed with personality from mere things, we find it surprisingly easy to distinguish between chairs, tables, pens, and speaking computer systems on the one hand, and living beings such as frogs, birds, and humans on the other. A famous observation in the phenomenology of *Jean-Paul Sartre* is helpful in understanding this paradoxical situation. With his description of the "gaze," he points out that we identify someone as a person based on the assumed possibility of falling into their *gaze* (cf. Sartre, 1943/1991, p. 457ff.). In this way, unlike with any other *thing*, we intuitively assume that a person has their own perspective on us, the world, and other people. A person always takes the world into their own *view* in this way. It is important for our investigation that Sartre does not start from a psychological observation at this point, because the gaze cannot be considered a behavior whose meaning we may have learned at some point or that is exclusively associated with the sense of sight. Even a blind person can take us *into their gaze*. We must therefore understand the gaze as a perspectival prerequisite for dealing with the world, which we attribute to those beings whom we can encounter as more than mere things.

One can understand the category of gaze also in the extended sense that it can not only be applied to humans, but already marks the difference between living beings and mere objects. We do not talk to our hats, but with our pets, and assume that our dog looks at us and reacts to our words from its own inner perspective. A mental dysfunction like visual agnosia, as described by *Oliver Sacks*, not only shows the problems that arise when we lack the ability to distinguish between things and soulful beings (cf. Sacks, 2015). Indeed, having a "soul" is the term to identify this specific perspective. Aristotle already makes this determination and designs in his writing *De Anima*, which *Klaus Corcilius* refers to as his "metaphysics of the living" (cf. Aristotle, 350 BC/2017, p. XX), a non-empirical concept of the soul. We cannot grasp the soul like a thing and yet we must accept it in the body as given when we identify a living being as alive. Then we accept it as the instance that regulates the functions of the organs and nutrition, the movements and in an intelligent being like the human, the inner dialogue and the own perspective as an individual. In this way, we can apply a concept of the *soul* that is not to be seen as a separate substance that stands in contrast to our body, but rather as an integrated example of the control of the physical actions of living beings. This metaphysics of ensoulment is by no means religious or irrational, as it may appear at first glance. Rather, it describes our everyday pragmatism of distinguishing between simple objects and living beings, to which we approach with different ways of thinking because we intuitively apply different transcendental concepts suitable for interaction with different parts of reality.

From this perspective, it initially seems incomprehensible why we should attribute a personality to something as artificial as brands. After all, brands do not act and react like the people we meet and greet on the street. On the other hand, we have the strong intuition that we indeed face brands as if they were persons. Thus, we can understand Aaker's talk of the *soul of the brand* (Aaker 1996, p. 45) just as well as the idea that successful brands are "those that have a soul" (Mathews-Wadhwa 2013), and that it is generally a good idea to "view brands as sentient beings", as brand pioneer *Hans Domizlaff* (1939/2005, p. 102) emphasizes.

As much as we might want to view statements like these as a kind of metaphorical speech, it would be difficult for us to refer to what could be meant by the *soul of a brand* without referring to attributes of personalities. For a closer understanding of this, we need to take a step back. Just like our intuition about brand personality, we do not question most everyday assumptions because our intuitive metaphysics of hats, dogs, and other people works predominantly smoothly. Upon closer inspection, however, it becomes apparent how many unconscious beliefs flow into our immediately appearing intuitions. For example, we are accustomed to living in a world shaped by the scientifically substantiated distinction between animate things and inanimate material. This is reflected in our everyday attitudes, such as the separation of physical and psychological problems. For instance, most of us do not find it very helpful to consult an astronomer working in an observatory if we have questions about personal mood swings. On the other hand, we would not expect valid results if we asked a psychologist about the reason for the alternation of day and night. We naturally assume that physics cannot say much about a person's inner state, just as we would call it pure nonsense to ask a psychologist to explain the sunrise to us according to psychological patterns. This is absolutely certain and obvious to us because we have established and practically meaningful distinctions between physical and psychological issues. However, this state of sharp separation between psychological and physical phenomena is historically quite new. For the longest time in human history, it was assumed, on the contrary, that our natural environment and with it the movement of the sun is determined by divine beings whose psychologically based actions we experience every day. Examples include the Greek god *Helios* who rides on his chariot, or the monotheistic deity *Aton,* who was worshipped by Pharaoh Akhenaten in the fourteenth century BC.

This and countless other examples follow the same pattern of not viewing the cosmos from the perspective of empirical science, which deals with the physical laws of dead matter. Rather, for the longest time of his existence, man often approached his external world by applying the same transcendental categories as he did when dealing with other animated beings. Dealing with the world from this *animistic perspective* leads to the assumption that lightning and thunder are not a weather event or expression of the climate, but phenomena caused by the anger of a living being—a god. Therefore, man must appease the god to change the weather and prevent further anger, for example by making sacrifices and performing certain secret rituals. It is noteworthy that at this point, people revert to the same behavioral patterns they use in everyday life to elicit the goodwill of other people. Just as we sometimes prompt another person to present our requests, we can understand the prayer of the ancient priests or the *magic* they performed as an attempt to indirectly establish a personal relationship with the nature surrounding us. They, as the initiated, can read the visible natural phenomena as the physiognomy of the divine personalities, to which they react through action, just like they do to the emotionally colored looks of their fellow human beings.

It is important to recognize that this approach is indeed the best choice for viewing and addressing the problem from a pre-scientific perspective. Certainly, prayers and magic do not always work, and unlike scientific theories, an animistic worldview does not directly lead to knowledge that is helpful in the manufacture of mechanical tools. However, understanding phenomena beyond one's own power as caused by deities provides sense and meaning in the chaos of events and calms the emotional ambivalence that humans feel in the face of an unfathomably appearing environment. In this sense, the rituals of connecting with the gods provide a sense of orientation in the face of the arbitrariness of natural processes.

The connection between the two is created by the *myth,* which narratively interprets the world as a social drama of conflicting forces of living beings and thus appeals to human emotion. The philosopher *Ernst Cassirer* describes this mythical consciousness as a symbolic form, meaning that it is a—and indeed the fundamental—perspective of humans with a holistic claim to explain the world. (Cassirer, 1944/1967, p. VI ff.; cf. Recki, 2013,

p. 29 ff.). All myths have in common that they interpret the visible phenomena in the world according to their origins and touch humans emotionally. Lightning and thunder as expressions of divine wrath shake us internally, and those who believe in the predestination of fate or certain individual fateful episodes by divine providence do not use cold analytical reason, but are guided by the consciousness of emotional agitation.

Returning to the problem of brand building, we can initially state that animism, mythology, and magic have not disappeared with the advancement of technology. We can illustrate this, for example, with astrology, whose status as a pseudoscience is based on the blurring of physical and psychological world views. Here, as with early humans, a certain behavior of things in the world is assumed, to which we can react in our own actions. The same applies to certain everyday objects, as *Karl Marx* already emphasized, who can certainly be considered an early "brand expert" (cf. Zschiesche & Errichiello 2018, p. 21). Thus, Marx speaks of a "mystical character" in relation to the world of goods, which goes hand in hand with the transformation of raw material into a commodity (Marx 1867/1962, p. 85). As a result of this transformation, we no longer view them as mere things to which we attribute a use value. Rather, we reflect ourselves and our culture in our goods and build a relationship with them that resembles religious idolatry. In this relationship, the commodity appears similar to the "endowed with its own life" (ibid.) sculpture in the animistic context—like a religious fetish, and thus becomes a commodity fetish.

Just as one might onomatopoeically call the legendary *Citroën DS* "la déesse", the goddess, and *Roland Barthes* describes it in his myths of everyday life as an angel fallen from heaven (cf. Barthes, 1957/2010, p. 196ff.), branded products play a special role in terms of commodity fetishism. They are designed to evoke a mythical-emotional engagement. From the perspective of a transcendental analysis, it is important to recognize that the connection between brand image and brand history established through branding follows the same structure as the mythical interpretation of the world. We experience brands through the products as immanent sensory phenomena, accompanied by narratives that explain their role in the world and promote emotional bonds. It is very revealing to see how we often forget that these stories are embellished by other people, if not entirely invented, with the aim of winning us over as customers. In relation to religious mythology, Cassirer calls this phenomenon an "unconscious fiction" and means that people only truly believe in their myths because they have forgotten that all gods and all stories about them were created by humans themselves:

> "Though myth is fictitious, it is an unconscious, not conscious fiction. The primitive mind was not aware of the meaning of its own creations." (Cassirer 1944/1967, p. 74).

At this point, Cassirer refers to a forgetting of the origin of the myth over generations; however, the emphasis on the unconscious also applies to all other forms of forgetting, repressing, or even actively neglecting the genesis of the myth. The only way to wholeheartedly believe in the story about the wrath of the god or any other myth is to regard the myth as the true truth and not as a narrative invented by humans with dubious validity.

It is precisely this feeling of the truthfulness of the myth that forms the core of the relationship to brands to which we attribute human-like personalities. Given the fact that traditional mythology has given way to a modern world of life with scientific explanatory models, it also becomes apparent in the face of brands how much we want to believe in the substantial truth of the myth *want*. Nothing is happening here in secret. One can always take a step back and become aware of the origin of the brand story as conscious storytelling and a product of a division of labor culture industry. At least with the brand products we favor, however, we seem to want to identify so much with the corresponding personality that we willingly ignore their existence as a targeted expression of creativity and strategy.

For an explanation of this perspective, we should ask about the benefit that leads to entering into an intimate relationship that goes beyond mere knowledge of facts. In this context, the anthropological concept of *relief* by the German philosopher *Arnold Gehlen* is helpful (cf. Waller, 2015). With this multidimensional term, he also describes that due to the complexity of the world, humans must not only have an objectifying rational approach to things, but also establish a reliable emotional connection to the world itself. Following this thought, animism, religion, astrology, and all other forms of mythical consciousness can provide such relief. Even if myth and magic do not yield immediately instrumentally usable success in dealing with the forces of nature, they still bring with them the psychological relief inherent in them, to stand on an equal footing with the sensually perceptible phenomena.

For both Gehlen and Cassirer, it is essential that it is characteristic of the myth to perceive the will of the deity quite *obviously* in the external appearances. In contrast to this idea, Gehlen provides enlightening considerations that modern empirical sciences indeed rely on observational data, but in the degree of abstraction of theories, they constitutively move in non-illustrative spheres. The modern human has gained an unprecedented degree of power over environmental threats in the scientific-technical world; at the same time, however, he must deal with the accompanying uncertainty that he can no longer rely on his own observation. Although, for example, looking into the twilight *obviously* shows us, the sun neither rises nor sets. We certainly do not deal with a deity in a golden chariot, but with a star of finite lifespan, around which our planet orbits in an elliptical path hidden from our immediate view. Even though none of us knows this orbit from our own observation, it is just as much a part of our reality as the optically hidden collision of electrons in a particle accelerator. This awareness, not being able to rely directly on one's own senses in the grand scheme of things, is, according to Gehlen's certificate, a serious psychological burden for modern humans. Insecurity and alienation in modern times are not only due to changing work and exploitation conditions, but also due to the perspective on the world that is largely closed to observation.

Relief through the myth of brands, as we can realize in light of this, also arises from the fact that they, as ever, push us into a world of projections of human personality heightened into the superhuman. In the cosmos of brands, we are once again surrounded by beings on an equal footing, who, moreover, are well-disposed towards us according to the immediate appearance of their beautiful form (cf. Vollbrecht, 2002, p. 774). We can hardly resist this impression of a relief that does not require further explanation through their messages, especially with the large global brands. Their apparent approachability constitutes a large part of the appeal of the lifestyle of the globalized middle class.

With this in mind, brands can ultimately be described as products of an ambivalent relationship, as Freud assumed it to be characteristic for religions. Just as, for example, the god of storms is supposed to protect us from the devastation of those typhoons that he himself has created, the personalities of strong brands relieve us from the burdens of precisely that globalized economy that has brought about this pressure (cf. Freud 1922, p. 25ff.). Brand myths can thus not only be understood as the brackets that hold together diverse products in various markets (cf. Gerken 1994). They also go a bit beyond the relationship between consumers and certain products and convey a more general, relieving feeling of living in a world where the need for security, belonging, appreciation, and self-realization can also be satisfied by the mere existence of certain brands.

The brands discussed in the following case studies serve as examples of these reliefs, in that they represent our brand-dominated world in a way that goes beyond their clientele. It is not always about revealing the mythical dimension of the brand in certain narratives. Rather, the mythical element is also evident in the fact that our interaction with brands proves to be compatible with patterns of thought that we use and need to interpret our world.

References

Aristoteles (2017). *Über die Seele.* Felix Meiner Verlag. (Originalwerk veröffentlicht circa 350 v.Chr.).
Aaker, D. A. (1996). *Building strong brands.* Free Press.
Azoulay, A., & Kapferer, J.-N. (2003). Do *Brand Personality Scales Really Measure Brand Personality?* Journal of Brand Management, 11(2), 143–155.
Barthes, R. (2010). *Mythen des Alltags.* Suhrkamp Verlag. (Originalwerk veröffentlicht 1957).
Burmann, C., Halaszovich, T. & Hemmann, F. (2012). *Identitätsbasierte Markenführung. Grundlagen – Strategie – Umsetzung – Controlling.* Springer Fachmedien.
Cassirer, E. (1967). *An Essay on Man. An Introduction to a Philosophy of Human Culture.* Yale University Press. (Originalwerk veröffentlicht 1944).
Domizlaff, H. (2005). *Die Gewinnung des öffentlichen Vertrauens.* Marketing Journal. Gesellschaft für angewandtes Marketing mbH. (Originalwerk veröffentlicht 1939).
Fioroni, M. & Titterton, G. (2009). *Brand Storming.* Palgrave.
Gerken, G. (1994). *Die fraktale Marke.* Econ Verlag.
Freud, S. (1922). *Totem und Tabu. Einige Übereinstimmungen im Seelenlebem der Wilden und Neurotiker.* Internationaler Psychoanalytischer Verlag.
Kant, I. (1990). *Kritik der Urteilskraft.* Felix Meiner Verlag. (Originalwerk veröffentlicht 1790).
Kniazev, M., & Belk, R. W. (2015): *Verpackung als Mittel zur Mythologisierung der Marke.* In: J. E. Schroeder (Hrsg.), *Brands: Eine interdisziplinäre Perspektive.* Oxon (CN). Routledge.
Marx K. (1962). *Das Kapital. Kritik der politischen Ökonomie. Erster Band. Buch I: Der Produktionsprozeß des Kapitals.* In: Institut für Marxismus-Leninismus beim ZK der SED (Hrsg.), Karl Marx Friedrich Engels Werke (MEW) (Bd. 23). Dietz Verlag. (Originalwerk veröffentlicht 1867).
Mathews-Wadhwa, A. (9.1. 2013). *Getting to the soul of your brand.* Forbes. http://www.forbes.com/sites/85broads/2013/01/09/getting-to-the-soul-of-your-brand/#254a51ba7477.
Nadeau, R. A. (2007). *Living Brands.* McGraw Hill Professional.

Qyll, N. (2021). *Visual Personal Branding. Eine frame-analytische Betrachtung ikonischer Personenmarken.* Herbert von Halem Verlag.
Recki, B. (2013). *Cassirer.* Reclam.
Sacks, O. (2015). *The Man Who Mistook His Wife for a Hat.* Pan Macmillan.
Sartre, J.-P. (1991). *Das Sein und das Nichts.* Rowohld Verlag. (Originalwerk veröffentlicht 1943).
Vollbrecht, R. (2002). *Marken, Mythen, Images: Über die Ko-Evolution von Werbung und Verbrauchern und die Figur des Re-Entrys in der Werbung,* in H. Willems (Hrsg.), *Die Gesellschaft der Werbung: Kontexte und Texte, Produktionen und Rezeptionen, Entwicklungen und Perspektiven* (S. 771–783). Westdeutscher Verlag.
von Bismarck, O., & Baumann, R. (1995). *Markenmythos: Verkörperung eines attraktiven Wertesystems.* Europäische Hochschulschriften.
von Uexküll, J. (1921). *Umwelt und Innenwelt der Tiere.* Springer Verlag.
Waller, S. (2015). *Leben in Entlastung. Mensch und Naturzweck bei Arnold Gehlen.* UVK Verlag.
Zschiesche, A. & Errichiello, O. (2018). *Marke statt Meinung.* GABAL Verlag.

Contents

1	**Apple: Magic Devices**	1
	References	8
2	**McDonald's: A Glorious Name**	11
	References	19
3	**Huawei: China's Promise**	21
	References	29
4	**Barack Obama: Back to the Future**	31
	References	41
5	**Fridays For Future: Genuine Authenticity**	43
	References	51
6	**BP: On This Side of Good and Evil**	53
	References	61
7	**Opel: Who We Are**	63
	References	72
8	**Beyond Meat: What We Should Eat**	75
	References	84

9	Boy London: The Logo is the Brand	87
	References	95
10	Bored Apes & Co: NFTs and Art as a Brand	97
	References	108

Afterword 111

About the Author

Prof. Dr. Stefan Waller is the Vice Dean of the Joint Institute of Zhejiang Wanli University and Brand University of Applied Sciences in Ningbo, China. From 2007 to 2013, he was a research associate at the Philosophical Seminar of the University of Hamburg and has been a Professor of Intercultural Brand and Innovation Culture at the Brand University of Applied Sciences in Hamburg since 2018. Since 2022, he has been living and teaching in Ningbo.

1

Apple: Magic Devices

Abstract Like few other brands, Apple has understood how to imbue itself and its products with a mythical aura. Stemming from the biography of its charismatic founder, the core of this brand's myth is that a mediation between technology and human nature is possible. This image corresponds with the magic of Apple devices, which lies in establishing an intuitive closeness to the world of modern technology.

The myth of *Prometheus* is one of the oldest explanations for the fact that humans are the animal not adapted to any specific environment, having to find their own way in the world. In the face of their lack of resources, they needed the help of a demigod to assert themselves in the world through the technology of fire, which has proven to be a tremendous developmental advantage over all other life forms. The ancient myth provides an answer to why humans, in their essentially deficient initial situation, are constitutively designed to constantly exceed the previously existing limits of what is possible through an excess of inventiveness. *Sigmund Freud* once called humans, in the consciousness of the accompanying psychological ambivalence, a "prosthetic god" (Freud, 1930/1997, p. 222), and indeed it is the technical aids that make our lives easier and at the same time constantly burden us. Thus, the most serious problems of the present no longer lie in overcoming any natural uncertainties such as warding off dangerous animals or dealing with uncertain weather conditions when discovering new continents. Rather, it is technology itself that has almost completely interposed itself between humans and first-hand nature, and thus, as *Hannah Arendt* puts it,

© The Author(s), under exclusive license to Springer-Verlag GmbH, DE, part of Springer Nature 2025
S. Waller, *Brand and Myth*, https://doi.org/10.1007/978-3-662-70678-7_1

increasingly turns us into a "switching animal" (Arendt, 1958/1981, p. 139) with a shell made of the technical devices surrounding us. In view of this, it proves to be a prominent task of architecture and design to create emotional closeness to this self-made second nature, which has often become alien to us and thus stands before us as inscrutable and threatening as the wild nature once did.

The company *Apple* was founded on April 1, 1976 by *Steve Jobs, Steve Wozniak* and *Ronald Wayne* with a starting capital of 1300 US$ in a garage in Silicon Valley. Ronald Wayne leaves the company early, which in its initial phase is shaped by Wozniak as the creative tinkerer and Jobs as the brilliant visionary with a feel for marketing. After the joint overwhelming success of the Apple II, the spectacular launch of Macintosh and Mac OS in 1984 and the subsequent sales weakness, the company parts ways with Steve Jobs. Apple then finds itself in an economic downturn that almost ends in bankruptcy. Only after Jobs' return in 1996 and the subsequent realignment of the company's management and product range can the company build on its previous successes. With the introductions of iPod (2001), iPhone (2007) and iPad (2010), these are then surpassed many times over. Steve Jobs dies in October 2011, leaving behind one of the most successful companies and one of the most valuable brands in the world.

This narrative of the brilliant company leader, whose career begins in a garage and who, after the first overwhelming success, is banished from the yard, undergoes trials and, after years of purification, leads the company to unprecedented achievements, only to not be able to enter the promised land of future greatness lying before him, could not have been better invented. Its fascination is not only due to the almost biblical dimension from today's perspective, but above all to the fact that it corresponds in many respects to the stages of a hero's journey described by *Joseph Campbell*. In his study *The Hero with a Thousand Faces* (Campbell, 1949/2004), Campbell addresses the question of what rules the standard course of mythical narratives follows. By demonstrating an exemplary course based on various myths and their heroes, according to Campbell, the actual myth is also only a single one. This monomyth describes the *thousand faces* of its heroes as the universal *coming of age* of a single hero's journey, which can roughly be divided into the three acts "departure into the unknown", "initiation" and "mature return":

> "The standard path of the mythological adventure of the hero is a magnification of the formula represented in the rites of passage: separation—initiation—return; which might be named the nuclear unit of the monomyth." (Ibid., p. 23).

The punchline of the journey in all cases is that mistakes, uncertainties and obstacles must be understood as necessary steps of a maturation process, which concludes in the sense of a return to oneself with the finding of the authentic self.

It is no secret that Hollywood productions are significantly influenced by this model. In addition to literally a thousand other film heroes, the appeal of characters like Luke Skywalker, Frodo Baggins and Harry Potter lies in our preference for this narrative form of the progressing *character arcs*. These heroes find early predecessors in German Romanticism, such as in Gottfried Keller's novel *Green Henry*, which is based on progress motifs that also appear in *G.W.F. Hegel's* philosophy of history. Both, like many Hollywood films, share the idea that the event may feel random in the experienced moment, but it can actually be a meaningful moment of a larger whole.

That he wants his own life story to be understood as such a significant journey, which was still ongoing at that time, is emphasized by Steve Jobs in his address to graduates of Stanford University in June 2005. The successful and famous CEO, who ended his own college career early, pays particular attention to his own departure into the unknown, which began with his separation from Apple:

> "I'm pretty sure none of this would have happened if I hadn't been fired from Apple. It was awful tasting medicine, but I guess the patient needed it." (Steve Jobs, quoted from Schlender & Tetzeli, 2016, p. 320).

Following the logic of the hero's journey, Jobs ultimately serves the romantic notion in this speech that there was an inner meaning in the sequence of life events, which he could only recognize in retrospect. "The owl of Minerva begins its flight only with the onset of dusk" (Hegel Works, Vol. 7, p. 14), Hegel summarizes this in a famous statement about world history as a Bildungsroman, for which Jobs in turn uses the image of retrospectively connecting decisive biographical points—"connecting the dots" (Schlender & Tetzeli, 2016, p. 318).

It is crucial that the insight into the inner meaningfulness of certain events is not suitable as a guide for the future: "You can't connect the dots looking forward; you can only connect them looking backward." (Ibid.). In order to make the right decisions in the here and now in a state of relative ignorance, one only has recourse to an authentic *self*: "You have to trust in something—your gut, destiny, life, karma, whatever." (Ibid.). The concluding slogan "Stay hungry, stay foolish" (ibid., p. 322) of his famous Stanford Commencement Speech is to be understood as the indispensable mode of this authentic striving.

"Unsatiated like the flame" (Nietzsche KSA 3, p. 367), could be the supplementary motto. Indeed, this speech about hunger and folly reminds us of *Friedrich Nietzsche* and his idea of the strong and creative individual, who sets himself apart from the masses by recourse to his own natural and unsocialized being. In his emphasis on life hunger and folly, Jobs actually agrees with Nietzsche that anyone who wants to grow beyond themselves in the sense of maximizing their own potentials must not ignore their irrational impulses. Natural drives, irrational ideas, and a researching spirit, as Nietzsche and Jobs show, are not opposites, but complement each other in an authentic self, which can only achieve great things by trusting in this authenticity:

> "We must discover the hero and also the fool who is in our passion for knowledge, we must occasionally become happy about our folly in order to remain happy about our wisdom!" (Nietzsche KSA 3, p. 464).

However, with regard to the brand, it falls short to relate this myth of the authentic self solely to the person Steve Jobs as the hero of the story. Its subject is also his life's work and thus essential for the Apple brand. Like every myth, the success story offers a biographically colored answer to the question of the origin and being of its subject, which is that Apple devices are always technically up-to-date and promote creativity in a unique way because through them the authentic and sometimes daring striving and genius of their founder works—which can be seen not least in the fact that the company almost went under without his help.

An exaggerated impression of the actual dire situation at Apple without Steve Jobs is conveyed by a scene from a 1996 episode of The Simpsons, in which *Homer Simpson* in a record store during a conversation with young people encounters complete ignorance about who Steve Jobs was and what an Apple computer is supposed to be (cf. Forrester & Archer, 1996). Immediately after rejoining as CEO of the high-tech company, Jobs counters this forgetfulness by highlighting the close connection between myth, man, and brand with the 1997 launched advertising campaign "Think different". This is a slogan that, due to its idiosyncratic grammatical form, seems to unite the highlighted synthesis of creative madness and wisdom. Apple does not think grammatically correct *differently*, but *different*—and with this peculiar use of words underlines the claim to go its own way in the entire approach to thinking. The brand feels connected to all those who change the world by disregarding the narrow-mindedness and conformity of those contemporaries for whom grammatical correctness is more important than creative ideas.

Indeed, it can be said that with the spot "The Crazy Ones," which is part of this campaign and thematizes this connection, Jobs anticipated the *points extended into the future* that he later apostrophized in the Stanford speech, thus anticipating not only the future success of the brand, but also the myth of his own person. Thus, the advertising campaign, with a voice-over to cinematic black-and-white shots of historical figures, invites us in a kind of prayer to trust the heroes of modernity and Apple with them:

"Here's to the crazy ones. The misfits. The rebels. The troublemakers. The round pegs in the square holes. The ones who see things differently. They're not fond of rules. And they have no respect for the status quo. You can quote them, disagree with them, glorify or vilify them. But the only thing you can't do is ignore them. Because they change things. They push the human race forward. And while some may see them as the crazy ones, We see genius. Because the people who are crazy enough to think they can change the world, Are the ones who do." (Think Different, 2023)

Although Steve Jobs does not appear in the line of positively *crazy* geniuses like Albert Einstein, Bob Dylan, Martin Luther King Jr., Mahatma Gandhi, Amelia Earhart, Alfred Hitchcock, Martha Graham, Frank Lloyd Wright, Pablo Picasso, and many others, it is also clear that he positions the brand as an advocate of rebellious geniuses because he counts himself among these extraordinary people.

Whether he was already aware at this time of the possible difference between himself and a similar, larger-than-life mythical persona Steve Jobs, who could easily be included here, cannot of course be said. However, an awareness of this emerges in the fact that an unpublished version of the aforementioned spot is spoken by Jobs himself, but in the published version by *Richard Dreyfuss* (cf. Golub et al., 1997). It would probably have been too much. In Jobs' original voice, it sounds almost blasphemous. It sounds as if the company leader, who was soon to be elevated to the Prometheus of our day, the iGod (cf. Lam, 2007), was addressing himself in a prayer.

A similar contribution to the construction of a larger-than-life heroic figure is made by the regular product presentations, which are even listed with their own Wikipedia article as "Stevenotes" (cf. Stevenote, 2023). These product shows, which were published early on in live stream, follow a fixed liturgy in which Steve Jobs takes on the role of the CEO in priestly form. If he still comes across a bit disguised, sometimes confirmation-like and with broad shoulder pads and bow tie almost clownish in earlier presentations, from the beginning of the 2000s with black *Issey Miyake* turtleneck, blue *Levi's* jeans, gray *New Balance* sneakers of the 991 series and the rimless Lunor glasses by *Robert Marc* (cf. Lynch, 2018, p. 142) the appropriate dress is also found. This outfit makes Jobs an icon of pop culture, perfectly matched to the reflexive relationship between persona and products. Sneakers and jeans stand for playful openness, for new ideas and trends as well as the hunger for change of a startup manager from Silicon Valley, and the modernized versions of existentialist top and nickel glasses for the intellectual claim of the now technically mature products.

Of course, these events are not only about the introduction of new products, but also about self-assurance and thus, like any ritual, about reviving and confirming the traditional. This claim may seem strange for a brand dedicated to technological progress and innovation. However, it shows that precisely because of the fast pace of the technological sector, occasions are necessary to reassure oneself of one's own strength at regular intervals. With this staging, Steve Jobs is the guarantor that the community—in a traditional sense—can expect nothing less than *magical* new products from the Apple brand. His appearances are flanked by the detailed reports of individual managers of the corporation, with Jonathan "Jony" Ive, then Chief Design Officer of Apple, not only achieving iconic status as a kind of altar boy in the form of a sidekick through language and gesture. He also takes on the role of the *primus inter pares* of Apple employees, by establishing a connection to the casual appearance of the sales staff in the Apple stores with his not Prussian blue, but just as simple T-shirts.

As a fixed part of the ritual, the announcement "One more thing…" borrowed from the legendary TV detective Colombo regularly follows the presentation of the latest innovations since the late 1990s. With this, Steve Jobs transitions to the presentation of the latest *magic device*—a technical achievement that overshadows everything previously thought possible. Given the development department at Apple, which does not stand still in the background, we know that the respective new gadget is technically outdated at the time of its presentation; however, the ritual itself is capable of giving the respective new device the aura of the magical and extraordinary. When Steve Jobs announces the new device with the timbre of serious emotion and holds it in his hands a little later, we have reached the end of history for a brief magical moment of perceived eternity. *We only need to connect the dots in retrospect to feel that everything that has been so far inevitably culminates in exactly this device.*

In addition to this staging, however, there is another reason to speak of the magic of the device, because humans have always had a technical relationship with magic, in the sense that magic is not about the application of physical laws, but about the will and social bonds. It is the achievement of myth that one's own will can relate to the external phenomena of the environment, such as other people, through magic. In the essentially technically crafted world of modern humans, however, this environment consists to a considerable extent of technical devices with which we must cope. The magic of Apple products thus consists in being aligned with each development step in an ever newer, better way to the user's field of vision, sense of touch, and voice, so that the user repeatedly gets the feeling of being able to communicate with the technically crafted world in a magical way through interaction with them. In conjunction with the magic invoked in the presentation, it is the ever more immediate communication with technology through ever more invisible apparatuses that establishes a magical aura of the devices themselves. An extension of the technical development steps into the future makes it unmistakably clear that the ultimate Apple product will connect directly with our thoughts without any external detours in the not too distant future. Where tactile elements have disappeared more and more with *Siri, AirPods* and facial recognition, the presentation of the VR glasses *Apple Vision Pro* in June 2023 seems to open up a new world in which we communicate with technology simply by looking at it.

Its ability, which shines through here, to sustainably change the deficient being human and his world through ever new prostheses, the company has already proven with the introduction of the iPad in 2010. Holding the new device of a completely new product class like Moses holding the tablets of commandments, the *character arc* of Steve Jobs closes. Indeed, the moment of the iPad presentation is very similar to a biblical narrative. The company leader, already marked by illness, fully slips into the role of the prophet by presenting a glowing tablet to the astonished congregation that shows them the future. Despite the greatest profits in the company's history (cf. Statista, 2018) after this, the perceived stagnation of the Apple brand is often attributed to Jobs' death in 2011: "This is no longer the Apple of Steve Jobs, when it could release epoch-shifting products every two years or so," is a relevant comment at Forbes (cf. Su, 2013).

With regard to the importance for the brand, it does not matter whether comments of this kind hit the core of the problem. It is also not relevant whether the actual life story of Steve Jobs justifies this close connection between personal genius and successful product range. It is also not important that friends and family members have different memories of Steve Jobs than the image conveyed in the biographies and biopics published after his death. For example, Jony Ive is very critical of the distorted image of Steve Jobs in the film of the same name (Boyle, 2015; cf. Makarechi, 2015).

On the other hand, it can hardly be denied that the general assumption about his character and the strong connection between the larger-than-life persona *Steve Jobs* and the brand *Apple* is the product of the enormous marketing talent of the Apple founder himself. His life story has long since become a globally accepted narrative, the authenticity of which could not be questioned by the fact that it is loosely based on factual events. It is indeed a modern myth in that its fictional elements are unproblematic for the broad masses.

With this glorification of the person, different *reliefs* through the myth of the Apple brand go hand in hand. First, there is the relief of the decision-making process when buying technology. Instead of venturing into the confusing market with various providers, there is great trust that the devices of this brand meet the highest standards of quality and innovation, because they are imbued with the creativity of a genius of the century. Apart from this, however, a relief not related to the purchase decision can also be identified, which also affects those people who would never buy a product of this brand. One only has to realize that owning an Apple device is not necessary to participate in the story of the college dropout becoming the CEO of one of the most innovative companies in the world. In a technical-practical sense, the touchscreen function was adopted by other manufacturers and in application areas beyond the iPhone and iPad. In this way, it has become a new element life in the repertoire of the communicative behavior of Homo sapiens, relieving everyday life in the world he has technically crafted. Above all, the Apple myth stands for the relieving feeling of living in a world where technology does not confront us as alien and threatening, but its development can be understood as a retrospectively meaningful process, the goal of which is the expansion of human potentials.

References

Arendt, H. (1981). *Vita Activa – oder vom tätigen Leben*. R. Piper & C. Verlag (Originalwerk veröffentlicht 1958).
Boyle, D. (2015). *Steve Jobs*. Universal Pictures.
Campbell, J. (2004). *The Hero With a Thousand Faces*. Princeton University Press (Originalwerk veröffentlicht 1949).
Forrester, B., & Archer, W. (Directors). (19 May 1996). *Homerpalooza*. In Groening, M. (Executive Producer), *The Simpsons,* Season 7, Episode 24.

Freud, S. (1997). *Das Unbehagen in der Kultur*. In A. Mitscherlich, A. Richard, & J. Strachey (Eds.), Ders., *Studienausgabe, Bd. IX. Fragen der Gesellschaft, Ursprünge der Religion* (pp. 191–270). Fischer (Originalwerk veröffentlicht 1930).

Golub, J., Schulman Edelstein, J., & Smith, C. Y. (1997). The Crazy Ones (Steve Jobs Version). https://www.youtube.com/watch?v=-z4NS2zdrZc. Accessed 20 Dec. 2023.

Hegel, G. W. F. (1986). *Werke in 20 Bänden, Bd. 7:* Suhrkamp. Grundlinien der Philosophie des Rechts.

Lam, B. (18 June 2007). IGod: Has Steve Jobs Peaked? https://gizmodo.com/igod-has-steve-jobs-peaked-269892. Accessed 20 Dec. 2023.

Lynch, K. (2018). *Steve Jobs*. White Lion Publishing.

Makarechi, K. (7. Oktober 2015). Jony Ive Calls Steve Jobs Movie a "Heartbreaking" Hijacking. https://www.vanityfair.com/news/2015/10/jony-ive-steve-jobs-movie-heartbreaking. Accessed 20 Dec. 2023.

Nietzsche, F. (1980ff). *Sämtliche Werke. Kritische Studienausgabe in 15 Bänden, herausgegeben von G. Colli and M. Montinari*. DTV de Gruyter. Zitiert als „KSA". – KSA 1, *Die Geburt der Tragödie* (Originalwerk veröffentlicht 1872). – KSA 3: Morgenröthe (Originalwerk veröffentlicht 1881).

Schlender, B., & Tetzeli, R. (2016). *Becoming Steve Jobs*. Hachette.

Statista. (2018), Apple's Revenue Worldwide From 2004 to 2018* (in billion U.S. dollars). https://www.statista.com/statistics/265125/total-net-sales-of-apple-since-2004/. Accessed 20 Dec. 2023.

Su, J.-B. (24 December 2013). Why Apple Lost its Innovation Spirit with New iPads. https://www.forbes.com/sites/jeanbaptiste/2013/10/23/apple-lost-innovation-spirit-with-new-ipads/. Accessed 20 Dec 2023.

Stevenote. (11 November 2023). https://en.wikipedia.org/wiki/Stevenote. Accessed 18 Dec. 2023.

Think Different. (9 November 2023). https://de.wikipedia.org/wiki/Think_Different. Accessed 18 Dec. 2023.

2

McDonald's: A Glorious Name

Abstract By establishing an immediate emotional connection to the consumer through names, the question arises as to what contribution the right name can make to the success of a brand. The history of the McDonald's restaurant chain shows that big brands are successful in part because their names have a fitting sound. However, it can also be observed that the magic of a big brand's name is less the reason and more the result of a brand's success.

Among the decisive developments in the philosophy of the twentieth century is the paradigm shift known as the *linguistic turn*, which assigns the study of language a leading role in philosophical debate. We should not merely consider language as a mere intermediary between human consciousness on the one hand and objects on the other. Rather, we can realize that it is through its internal connection that it creates the reality to which we consciously relate. "Language is the house of being," as the often-quoted statement by *Martin Heidegger* informs us (Heidegger, 1947/1976, p. 319). This existential significance of language for brands can be primarily read from their proper names—it is the brand names, logos, colors, typefaces, and all other brand characteristics that endure unchanged over time.

However, the analysis of proper names and their meaning poses a challenge for modern philosophy of language. The founding father of modern philosophy of language, *Gottlob Frege*, advocates a model that distinguishes between the *sense* and *meaning* of proper names (Frege, 1892/2019). Essentially, a proper name is a kind of placeholder for more complex facts, which we can understand as its *meaning* in a terminology somewhat contrary to our everyday language use. To hit the meaning of the intended, we can use the corresponding more complex expression instead of the proper name. Thus, we could replace McDonald's, for example, with the expression "largest restaurant chain in the world, measured by revenue in 2017" (cf. Forbes, 2017).

At first approach, this remark seems to be a universally applicable self-evidence, which is why we find it unproblematic in everyday life when we are informed about who or what is behind a certain name by referring to certain characteristics. However, the difficulty inherent in this one-sided view becomes clear when we refer, for example, to a truly familiar person. Thus, my wife is probably "the person I married on our wedding day". But when I call her by her name, I mean not only the meaning of this or any other biographical fact, but associate with the name itself a certain content. Frege summarizes this as the "sense" inherent in the proper name itself and distinct from the meaning (cf. Frege, 1892/2019, p. 11), the position of which between purely subjective conception on the one hand and meaning of the object on the other can be aptly illustrated by name changes. If names were merely arbitrary words for identifying certain subjects, then such a change would be about as relevant as always using an x instead of a u for a variable in an equation. In fact, however, name-givings and name changes are events of some significance, in which much more happens than that we attach certain designations to things and subjects. They give them a special, supra-subjective *sense*. In relation to a conception of language as the house of being, a person "is" this name in an existential sense from the moment of his naming, and a change affects him in his entire being.

A sign of this existential connection between proper names and people can also be seen in the fact that it makes it possible to change the world through mere expressions of will. This is the case, for example, when one asks someone for something and then does not have to do it oneself. By presupposing personalities, i.e., animate beings on the recipient side, the request when naming the name is the prototype of magic. This thought can be found, for example, in *Ernst Cassirer* in his considerations on myth. He points out that the otherwise alien nature becomes manageable from the perspective of mythical consciousness by calling the forces at work in it by their peculiar name:

> "Whoever knows the true name of a god or demon, therefore, also unreservedly owns the power of its bearer; an Egyptian tale tells how Isis, the great sorceress, tricks the sun god Ra into revealing his name to her, and how she thereby gains dominion over him and all other gods." (Cassirer, 1925/2002, p. 51 f.).

A strangely similar account of the magical power of the name can also be found in John Lee Hancock's film *The Founder* (2016), which tells the life story of the apostrophized McDonald's founder *Ray Kroc*. In fact, this story is not so dissimilar to that of the great sorceress *Isis*, in that Kroc, by purchasing the company, primarily seizes the brand name. According to the film's dramaturgy, his cunning lies in recognizing, unlike *Dick* and *Mac McDonald's* as the actual founders and first franchise givers of fast food restaurants, the decisive importance of the name for the success of the company. After the decisive company purchase, he reveals the reason, hitherto concealed from the cinema-goers, for buying the company and not simply copying its system:

"It's not just the system. It's the name. That name. That glorious name. McDonald. It's wide open. Limitless. It could be anything, whatever you want it to be. It sounds like... America." (Ray Kroc played by Michael Keaton in *The Founder* (Hancock, 2016)).

Indeed, this conversation between Ray Kroc and Richard McDonald, taking place in a men's restroom, is brilliant, especially with *Michael Keaton* being the ideal casting for a somewhat washed-up traveling salesman who only begins his life's work in the advanced second half of his life.

However, it is advisable to take a closer look at the *meaning* of the name McDonald's, because The Founder is largely about Ray Kroc and not just about the development of McDonald's. In the film's arc of suspense, the thing with the name is a very good punchline to illustrate Kroc's outstanding understanding of the effectiveness of a brand. However, it is questionable whether a name alone can explain the success of this or any other brand. Looking at many other successful brands, the aesthetic quality or cultural anchoring of a name seems to have little to nothing to do with the success of a brand in advance. Otherwise, it would be hard to explain why such an ordinary name as *Microsoft* for a software company or a brand reminiscent of cocaine for beverages are among the most successful brands in the world. Nevertheless, today probably no one will deny the effect of these names and will certainly admit that McDonald's is not only good, but the only suitable name for this restaurant chain listed in the top 10 of the most valuable brands worldwide.

A plausible explanation for the fact that we only make this evaluation retrospectively is the effect of habituation. We should not imagine names as mere labels for identifying entities, but as existentially connected with the life courses of the name bearers with whom we are dealing. With regard to the above-described *meaning* of a proper name, it could also be noted that parents have no choice but to give their children certain names relevant in their context (cf. Hornbostel, 1997). Correspondingly, positive as well as negative prejudices and expectations are associated with certain names in their respective context. For example, if you meet a child named *Emil* in the German-speaking world, you have a distinctly different idea of his parents' home than if it were a child named *Kevin*. In view of this, it can indeed be argued that McDonald's has an All-American name, the *meaning* of which is conducive to the brand's existence. Bearing in mind that it is not the only name with this characteristic, it also becomes apparent that the specific meaning of certain brand names, like natural persons, only crystallizes with the biographies of the name bearers. In the sense that a certain idea goes along with the name, in that the name is filled with life, it is likely that the specific meaning and thus the magic of a brand name like McDonald's only came about with the success of the company.

Following this process of crystallization, it should first be noted that Ray Kroc, according to his own statement and contrary to the film's dramaturgy, did not buy the company solely because of the name. Rather, his talent as an experienced traveling salesman and connoisseur of the practical side of the business is evident in the realization that acquiring the company provides a decisive development advantage over any copier. If he had merely copied the original *McDonald's-Speedy-System* like many others, he would have had to make all the big and small mistakes that the McDonald brothers had already made and eliminated over many years (cf. Love, 1986, p. 42). But this way, he was able to assert himself with a technically completely mature system in the already fiercely contested American market of fast food chains in the 1960s. From this point of view, the extreme degree of standardization of furnishings, workflows, and products is the essential characteristic of McDonald's everywhere in the world. In addition to the fact that the offer is actually identical everywhere except for a few country-specific extras, this high demand for uniform quality is evident, for example, in the so-called *Big Mac Index* (The Economist, 2023), which has been comparing the purchasing power of different currencies based on the price of a Big Mac in the respective national currency since 1986.

Due to the wide dispersion of its branches, McDonald's has been a part of many small communities in the USA from the beginning, as its affordable offerings made restaurant visits possible for the entire American nuclear family. McDonald's has early on reinforced this with marketing that is specifically tailored to families and children. The comic characters around Ronald McDonald, playgrounds, and child-friendly communication in the restaurants have contributed to being perceived as a family restaurant. Moreover, McDonald's is a meeting place for teenagers in rural areas, particularly in the absence of other options, many of whom take their first steps into the working world at McDonald's. Since the management of a McDonald's fast-food restaurant differs from all previously existing offerings in the restaurant industry, a separate academy for franchisees was established as early as the early 1960s. However, most tasks in the division of labor organized fast food restaurants do not require higher education. These simple jobs were exported abroad with the expansion of McDonald's that began in the 1970s, just like burgers and fries. In the increasingly globalized world of work, it is only logical that since 2012 there has been a *McJob-Index* (Hern, 2012), derived from the Big Mac Index, which compares the hourly wages for the completely identical work processes of over a million McDonald's employees worldwide.

A deeper societal anchoring of the fast food chain, which goes beyond what could be achieved through the ubiquity of affordable food, simple jobs, and clever marketing, was impressively demonstrated during the 1992 riots in Los Angeles. These riots, which predominantly affected the underprivileged black population, devastated large parts of downtown Los Angeles and were accompanied by destruction and looting of retailers and restaurants. To general astonishment, however, none of the McDonald's branches in the otherwise completely devastated zones of the hardest confrontations were affected. One reason for this is seen in the fact that the franchisees committed themselves to their community with small aids such as basketballs for teenagers and free coffee for the unemployed (cf. Ebeling, 2012). Apparently, they took to heart the motto given by Ray Kroc himself to give back part of their success to the community. This principle has been established since 1974 with the *Ronald McDonald House Charity* (Ronald McDonald House Charities, 2023). More important than this institution, however, appears to be the fact that the McDonald's franchisees, like elsewhere, come from the neighborhood itself and the respective restaurants are therefore perceived by the outraged masses as a part of their own environment worth protecting (cf. Harris, 2009, p. 70 ff.). A regional McDonald's manager noted, "people believe that you do not mess around where my son works, or with what my neighbor owns, or where my wife eats." (Ibid., p. 71). Ray Kroc's early insight that individually owned branches operate much more successfully than those with possibly non-local managers is reflected in this positive external perception.

The name McDonald's "sounds like America," as can be said about the magic it exudes up until the 1990s, because its entrepreneurial action is based on the ideal of the American dream, reconciling division of labor Fordism and entrepreneurial commitment in a capitalist system that does not lose its connection to the community. In this way, McDonald's is almost synonymous with the promises of the consumer society of ubiquitous availability of consistently high-quality affordable products, which the brand can connect with playful ease and the utopia of general welfare.

These progressive characteristics are succinctly captured in their differentiation from the competition with the slogan used in Germany in the 1970s, "The somewhat different restaurant" (cf. List of McDonald's marketing campaigns 2023). The slogan appeals to a generation that wants to do things differently than the previous one and is largely positive about globalization. Coca-Cola, Nike, Star Wars, and the presence of a McDonald's are for them the external signs of the increasingly becoming reality positive idea of a world completely integrated by the Western lifestyle, in which regional peculiarities can only be read in details—such as calling a "Quarter Pounder with Cheese" in Paris simply a "Royal," as we learn in *Quentin Tarantino's* masterpiece *Pulp Fiction* (1994).

With some justification, it can be argued that the word magic of McDonald's reaches a first peak in a phase of modernity in which this utopia seems to become reality with the presumed end of the greatest possible mythical narrative. Nothing less than the *character arc* of history itself seems to close in the 1990s, as the capitalist West triumphs over the socialist East, as *Francis Fukuyama* postulates in reference to the considerations of *G.W.F. Hegel* about the *end of history* (Fukuyama, 1992). Few images illustrate the intended triumph of the Western model over the Eastern Bloc states like the long lines in front of the first McDonald's branch in Moscow, which opened two years before the end of the Soviet Union on December 31, 1990 (cf. Althanns, 2007). The hope associated with the fall of the Iron Curtain that market economy cooperation would inevitably lead to peaceful coexistence is aptly formulated by *Thomas L. Friedman* with the "Golden Arches Theory" reminiscent of Kant's dictum of peace among democracies: "No two countries that both had McDonald's had fought a war against each other since each got its McDonald's" (Friedman, 1996). In a sense, the withdrawal of McDonald's from Russia in May 2022 provides a proof *ex negativo* of this theory (McDonald's, 2023).

From today's perspective, the upheaval in the early 1990s, which describes not the end but rather a turning point in history, has not been without consequences for McDonald's long before this event. With its expansion to India and China, the restaurant chain proves that a preference for American-style fast food is cross-cultural (cf. Mujtaba, 2007). At the same time, however, growing competition, problematic pricing policies, and above all the changing health consciousness in the USA lead to a drop in profits and a crash in the stock, which reaches its low point in 2002 with a loss of 39.25% (Macrotrends, 2020). At the same moment, McDonald's increasingly becomes a synonym for the fears of decline of the middle class. If it was always a difficult-to-fulfill utopia to connect the simple and monotonous work at McDonald's with the American dream, the term "McJob" now stands for any kind of unattractive, uncreative, poorly paid, and demeaning work in the globalized service sector (cf. Urban Dictionary, 2023).

In this situation, McDonald's launches its first global branding campaign in 2003, whose motto "I'm lovin' it", conceived by the German agency *Heye und Partner*, replaces the slogans that had previously differed in various countries. Worth mentioning is the approach of *transmedia storytelling* that was still unusual for the early 2000s, which goes beyond the medium of advertising. Thus, the slogan and jingle are not only used in the official advertising measures, but are also placed in a pop song of the same name by *Justin Timberlake*, which is released as a regular single at the same time as the campaign (cf. Hogan, 2016). Since the song is not clearly an advertising jingle, both the slogan and jingle gain a wider distribution and the campaign gains authenticity.

Not only is the song original enough to stand on its own, but in combination with the music video, it also provides the key to understanding the campaign. In the music video, the "it" is the "certain something" of an unknown girl, whom the singer spontaneously follows through the urban jungle. This action, which we would probably condemn as stalking today, was still unabashedly positive in 2003 as an expression of spontaneous trust in one's own feelings. Although less glamorous, the actors in the simultaneously running McDonald's commercials also have a sense for the "certain something" in life, by creatively and spontaneously transforming monotonous and complicated situations into special emotionally interesting events. The editing and tonality of the commercials unmistakably tie in with the aesthetics of the progressive film of the 1990s. However, its nihilistic to hedonistically frivolous rejection of normal life, as we know it from the opening monologue of the character Renton in Danny Boyle's *Trainspotting* (1996), turns into a passionately conformist affirmation. *I'm loving it* reflects the attitude of a fully adapted and thereby finding the special in the ordinary, which also includes the insignia of the McDonald's brand appearing in the film snippets.

The strategic approach of the campaign can thus be described as directly addressing the company's problems by dissociating any potential criticism of the products from the feeling for the brand. The special quality of McDonald's food takes a back seat in favor of the positive feeling associated with the brand. This approach becomes particularly apparent when the previous German-language slogans are used for comparison: "The somewhat different restaurant." "Eating with fun." "Good that McDonald's exists." "The place where you like to be because you eat well." "McDonald's is simply good." "Every time a good time." (List of McDonald's marketing campaigns, 2023). These slogans have in common that they refer to a specific aspect of the restaurant operation and thus also offer a target for criticism of this very aspect. They raise the question of whether everything at McDonald's is really just fun, everything is good, and whether you actually eat well. In the face of the pleasing *badabababa jingle*, these questions no longer arise because it already has the answer: *I'm loving it,* even if there might be something to criticize about the hamburger.

Certainly, Heye and Partner were not aware that Kant had developed a very similar contrast between positive feeling and rational evaluation with the theorem of *disinterested pleasure*. He argues for works of art that their beauty deserves appreciation, even if their genesis contradicts our idea of the good. A palace, for example, can still be beautiful even if it was built by a tyrant (cf. Kant, 1790/1974, p. 116). The criticism of this falls short with regard to the part of our consciousness responsible for the perception of beauty, because perceiving beauty is not affected by aversion to bad governance. Certainly, a *Big Mac* would hardly fall into the category of beauty according to Kant's standards. However, this is not the point, but rather the McDonald's brand, whose significance for the consumer can indeed be separated from the quality of the products. Even without having to answer the question of whether brands can be considered works of art in the same way as palaces, the success of the campaign suggests that there is a high willingness for an aesthetic attitude towards this brand that disregards many other aspects. Certainly, there were changes in the operational business as well as in the brand's appearance in the following decades, which responded to both the negative attitude towards fast food and the changing zeitgeist. The introduction of the *McCafés* in response to the coffee house trend led by Starbucks, as well as the focus on more sustainability and environmental awareness, and the associated use of green as a CI color in many countries, are outstanding innovations. These and many other changes have probably led to higher acceptance among environmentally and trend-conscious customers in Western societies. However, for the same clientele, McDonald's remains the epitome of unhealthy food and mass operation, as this problem is regularly addressed by investigative journalism (cf. Spurlock, 2004;

Sükar, 2019). In view of this, the strength of *I'm lovin' it* lies in the fact that McDonald's does not need to resolve the contradictions between fast food and healthy nutrition, precarious assembly line work and creative future perspectives, the American dream and the globalized reality, because we do not have to justify our feelings. Just as Renton in Trainspotting does not have to be impressed by arguments for an orderly life as long as he follows his feeling for a different lifestyle, *I'm lovin' it* encourages restaurant visitors to dine at McDonald's despite better knowledge because of the feeling for that special something. This is exactly why this slogan has reached a status today that is perhaps only surpassed by *Just Do It*.

It is probably not too much to say that the name McDonald's has thus experienced not a new meaning but a noticeable shift in its sense. It probably lies in the eye of the beholder whether McDonald's has thus earned an even more glorious name for itself. It might be more accurate to say that the name has a certain resonance that makes McDonald's the most valuable fast food brand in the world.

References

Althanns, L. (2007). Die Eröffnung des ersten McDonald's In Moskau. Themenportal Europäische Geschichte. https://www.europa.clio-online.de/essay/id/fdae-1412. Accessed 20 Dec. 2023.

Boyle, D. (1996). *Trainspotting*. Miramax Films.

Cassirer, E. (2002). *Gesammelte Werke*, Hamburg Meiner Verlag (ECW 12), darin: *Philosophie der symbolischen Formen, Zweiter Teil: Das mythische Denken* (Originalwerk veröffentlicht 1925).

Ebeling, C. (17 July 2012). Rodney King death today reminds of a positive lesson from LA riots. https://applewoody.wordpress.com/2012/06/17/rodney-king-death-today-reminds-of-a-positive-lesson-from-la-riots/. Accessed 20 Dec. 2023.

Forbes. (2017). McDonald's Is King of Restaurants in 2017. https://www.forbes.com/pictures/591c79084bbe6f1b730a5811/2017-global-2000-restaura/#78d-0bcc36d2a. Accessed 30 Aug. 2023.

Frege, G. (1892/2019). *Über Sinn und Bedeutung*. Philipp Reclam jun. Verlag.

Friedman, T. L. (8 Dec. 1996). Foreign affairs big mac. *The New York Times*. https://www.nytimes.com/1996/12/08/opinion/foreign-affairs-big-mac-i.html. Accessed 20 Dec. 2023.

Fukuyama, F. (1992). *The end of history and the last man*. Free Press.

Hancock, J. L. (2016). *The Founder*. The Weinstein Company.

Harris, P. S. (2009). *None of us is as good as all of us*. Wiley.

Heidegger, M. (1976). *Brief über den Humanismus, in ders., Wegmarken.* Klostermann (Originalwerk veröffentlicht 1947).

Hern, A. (22 June 2022). The McJob Index. https://www.newstatesman.com/blogs/economics/2012/06/mcjob-index. Accessed 20 Dec. 2023.

Hogan, M. (14 July 2016). The Contentious Tale of the McDonald's 'I'm Lovin' It' Jingle. Pitchfork. https://pitchfork.com/thepitch/1227-the-contentious-tale-of-the-mcdonalds-im-lovin-it-jingle/. Accessed 30 Aug. 2020.

Hornbostel, S. (1997). *Eigennamen – Die Politik der feinen Unterschiede.* In K.-S. Rehberg (Ed.), *Differenz und Integration: die Zukunft moderner Gesellschaften; Verhandlungen des 28. Kongresses der Deutschen Gesellschaft für Soziologie im Oktober 1996 in Dresden*; Band 2: Sektionen, Arbeitsgruppen, Foren, Fedor-Stepun-Tagung (pp. 407–414). Westd Verl.

Kant, I. (1974). *Kritik der Urteilskraf.* Suhrkamp (Originalwerk veröffentlicht 1790).

List of McDonald's marketing campaigns. (8 Dec. 2023). https://en.wikipedia.org/wiki/List_of_McDonald%27s_marketing_campaigns. Accessed 18 Dec. 2020.

Love, J. F. (1986). *McDonald's. Behind the Arches.* Bantam.

Macrotrends. (2020). McDonald's – 50 Year Stock Price History|MCD. https://www.macrotrends.net/stocks/charts/MCD/mcdonalds/stock-price-history. Accessed 30 Aug. 2020.

McDonald's. (16 May 2022). McDonald's to Exit from Russia. https://corporate.mcdonalds.com/corpmcd/our-stories/article/mcd-exit-russia.html. Accessed 24 May 2023.

Mujtaba, B. G. (2007). *McDonald's Success Strategy and Global Expansion Through Customer and Brand Loyalty.* Journal of Business *Case Studies, 3*(3), 55–66.

Nier, H. (2017). Wie lange man weltweit für einen Big Mac arbeiten muss. https://de.statista.com/infografik/9944/wie-lange-man-weltweit-fuer-einen-big-mac-arbeiten-muss/. Accessed 23 Dec. 2023.

Ronald McDonald House Charities. (23 Nov. 2023). https://en.wikipedia.org/wiki/Ronald_McDonald_House_Charities. Accessed 20 Dec. 2023.

Spurlock, M. (2004). *Super Size Me.* Samuel Goldwyn Films Roadside Attractions.

Sükar, H. (2019). *Die Fast Food-Falle: Wie McDonald's und Co. auf Kosten unserer Gesundheit Milliarden verdienen.* Edition a.

Tarantino, Q. (1994). *Pulp Fiction.* Miramax Films.

The Economist. (2023). Big Mac Index. http://www.economist.com/topics/big-mac-index. Accessed 23 Dec. 2023.

Urban Dictionary: McJob. (11 Dec. 2003). https://www.urbandictionary.com/define.php?term=McJob. Accessed 23 Dec. 2023.

3

Huawei: China's Promise

Abstract China's development over the past few decades is perceived from a Chinese perspective as a resurgence after a long period of national weakness. The brand Huawei embodies this as the promise of China's emancipation, arising from its own work, from being the world's workbench to becoming the leading economic nation of the 21st century. Therefore, the rise, fall, and resurgence of Huawei is a measure of the strength of Chinese technology and economic performance like no other brand.

By describing the journey of the monomythic hero as a personality development overcoming obstacles, as described by *Joseph Campbell*, the protagonist usually assumes the role of the underdog, from which the power of the existing must be overcome. Only when foreign forces are defeated and oppressive powers change for the better, can the purified return to oneself succeed. In the eschatological variant that all earthly constraints can be overcome as such, the narrative is an integral part of religious narratives (cf. Campbell, 1949/2008, p. 35). In a secular form, the narrative is found in the idea of the proletarian world revolution, which, contrary to religious notions of the afterlife, aims at improving the situation in this life. The line "You'll get pie in the sky when you die" in *Joe Hill's* song *The Preacher and the Slave* (Fowke, 1973, p. 155 ff.) ironically formulates what the socialist international brings forward with the seriousness of the battle song. It should be added that the capitalist dream of dishwasher to millionaire shares the same assessment. One should not leave one's own fate to foreign powers and promises of the afterlife, but can only change it for the better through one's own work here and now.

At a very abstract level, an analysis that significantly highlights the aspect of work as a key to overcoming existing conditions can already be found in the early nineteenth century in the description of the Master and Servant Dialectic in G.W.F. Hegel's epoch-making work *Phenomenology of Spirit* (Hegel Works, Vol. 7). In his own way of viewing world events from the head as the development of human self-consciousness, Hegel is not concerned with leveling material differences or the apotheosis of individual entrepreneurship. Rather, he wants to show how the asymmetric relationship of domination dissolves in the self-awareness and liberation of the servant arising from his work. In short, this can be described from the situation that servants do the work for the master. In this way, the master initially benefits from the fruits of their activity, but at the same time, the servants get to know the world by changing it through the work assigned to them. The compulsion to work thus leads to the master constantly alienating himself from the world in a continuous consumer attitude towards the processed goods, just as the servants get to know the world, as they become experts in all sorts of things through work. Hegel further describes that the master ultimately becomes superfluous in his role, because the consciousness of the servant, formed by the real problems, can orient itself independently in the world even without external compulsion. In truth, only a consciousness that has also taken the trouble to literally *get a hands-on understanding of the world* can move independently, i.e., free from external determination. Hegel therefore draws the following conclusion: "The truth of the independent consciousness is thus the servile consciousness." (Hegel Works, Vol. 7, p. 152).

Of course, the dialectic of domination and servitude plays a systematic role in Hegel's Phenomenology of Spirit and also has a prehistory, which we cannot follow in detail here. Apart from this, however, his version of this drama is inspiring in its own right, not least because it bears the traits of the mythical narrative of the victorious hero's journey of the supposedly weaker one. The points of connection to the working class as a historical subject also seem obvious, even though the left Hegelian *Karl Marx* himself never refers to this passage in Hegel (cf. Arthur, 1983). But the promise of success through one's own activity can also be applied to entrepreneurship under the conditions of the market economy. Not least, the narrative of the global triumph of the West before 1989 is based on the fact that the more efficient form of economy has also prevailed the more advanced form of productive work. In this sense, the Mercedes star, clearly visible from the east of the city on the Berlin Europa-Center at the time, symbolizes the superiority of German engineering skill, which is servilely integrated into the dictate of capitalism, over the work condemned to dependency in planned economic production conditions.

However, history did not come to an end in the early 1990s. Thus, the globalization gaining momentum in this decade is significantly associated with the fact that labor-intensive productive activities are being shifted from the West to countries with lower wages and a larger workforce in Asia—especially China. More precisely, the production sites are relocated to the Far East, while the intellectually demanding tasks for development, marketing and administrative activities, as well as the largest part of the profits, usually remain in the western home countries of global brands. The new border marked by free trade between East and West thus also becomes a separation between intellectual and manual activity.

A summary of this development in eight words can be found on the back of many Apple products: "Designed by Apple in California. Assembled in China." With the carefully chosen term "assembled," Apple has found a suitable linguistic regulation to avoid the long-time association of the term "Made in China" with cheap goods on its high-priced devices. Speaking of "assembled in China" neatly separates the mere executing work on the *assembly lines* of Chinese factories on the one hand, and the actual quality-creating creative performance of the corporation from California on the other. Apart from the fact that Apple's headquarters is indeed located in the state of California, the local framing refers to the myth of Silicon Valley and especially to Steve Jobs as a college drop-out in the creative scene of the westernmost state of the USA, influenced by the hippie movement. This differentiation is important for Apple's branding—it is the creative performance from California that refines the product and is responsible for a profit margin that pushes the share of material and production costs for an iPhone incurred in China to below 40% in the global value chain. (cf. Tuan Do, 2023).

It is certainly not an exaggeration to say that this relatively small share of the fruits of their own labor is due to the trauma of the decline that the Chinese nation experienced in the period known in history as the Century of Humiliation, from the first Opium War 1839-42 to the founding of the People's Republic of China on October 1, 1949 (cf. Kaufman, 2010). The efforts after the founding of the Republic of China and the successful economic rise as a result of the reform policy from the mid-1970s are accompanied by the narrative of overcoming this national humiliation; and also the government motto "Rejuvenation of the Chinese Nation" chosen by *Xi Jinping* at the beginning of his first term in 2012 (cf. Jacob & Hoang, 2020) refers to this motive for a resurgence of China. In recent times, in addition to initiatives such as the global *Belt-and-Road-Project*, Chinese technology manufacturers also play a prominent role in this national effort. The international success of young and progressive companies and brands is rightly seen as evidence of China's renewed economic strength and technical superiority.

Since these brands have mostly emerged in the environment of production facilities for foreign manufacturers, it can be said that the narrative of emancipation through self-education, as spelled out by Hegel, particularly applies to companies in the young megapolis *Shenzhen* in southeastern China. The telecommunications and consumer electronics manufacturer *Huawei* excellently demonstrates that the self-confidence of the Chinese nation is fed by the certainty of having educated and liberated itself through its own work. Thus, Huawei, along with *Xiaomi*, is one of the few Chinese brands in the *Interbrand Top-100-Ranking* of the world's most important brands in 2023 (Interbrand, 2023) and was even the smartphone manufacturer with the largest market share worldwide during the Corona crisis in 2020 (cf. Laricchia, 2023). The naming of the company is inextricably linked with China's expected rise. The name Huawei (华为) is derived from the well-known slogan in China "中华有为" (Zhonghua youwei), which translates as "China has great potential" or "China is capable and promising" (cf. Tech.Ifeng.com, 2013). Although this was a spontaneous decision without much thought, the naming directly refers to Huawei as an answer to the promise of China's technological and societal progress to be fulfilled.

Even though the patriotic motif in the name could suggest Chinese government influence on Huawei, this is categorically denied by the company's management (cf. Plummer, 2018, pos. 3507 ff.). No less plausible than Apple's start in a garage, on the other hand, is the narrative of the entrepreneur as an underdog, who founded the later global corporation in 1987 with the unimaginably small start-up capital of only 21,000 RMB (cf. Tao, 2014, p. XXVff.; Nylander, 2017, p. 45 ff.). The subsequent enormous success of the company suggests a hero's journey on the scale of a *Steve Jobs*—although the difference between the two founding personalities could hardly be greater. Ren is not a visionary youngster in worn-out jeans, but a veteran of the People's Liberation Army when he founded his company at the slightly advanced age of 42. Thus, *Tien Tao* describes him as someone who, although referred to by some as a kind of *Don Quixote*, pursued the rise of the company from the very beginning with a clear strategy. This approach, based on the learning processes of hard work, is to first take care of the unattractive places for the establishment of telecommunications technology that are little noticed by the large international corporations, and from there to approach the center of innovative business.

The first acts of Huawei's corporate history, which only started selling mobile phones under its own brand name from 2004, therefore do not unfold like Apple's as a public drama. Rather, the rise of the brand, which was already listed by Interbrand as a globally relevant top-100 brand from 2014, takes place *behind tthe scenes* of the world public. Huawei experienced its breakthrough in 1994 after a phase of reverse engineering of network technology with C&C08, a self-developed digital network switch (cf. Fan, 2006). The company can offer this for only two-thirds of the usual market price. The 2000s saw the expansion of operational business to Europe. There, in 2006, Huawei laid the foundation for its own international business with high-quality smartphones, specifically made for *Vodafone*. Already in the first year 2010, the company was able to sell 3 million smartphones. By the end of the fourth quarter of 2018, the benchmark of 200 million units sold was exceeded (Huawei Consumer BG, 2019).

From the hagiographic perspective of Tien Tao, this success of the company can be attributed primarily to the strong will of the founders born in the 1940s to 1950s (cf. Tao, 2014, p. XXV). This glorification of the chosenness of the generation born into the reform years includes both the reference to their patriotic and character ideals and the observation that this kind of dedication is largely no longer to be found in the now luxury-oriented Chinese present (cf. ibid., p. 132). It is certainly true that the beginnings were modest and memories such as those of makeshift mattress camps for the workers' lunch breaks in the factory belong to the myth of the rise associated with extreme willingness to perform (cf. ibid., p. 33). Ren Zhengfei highlights this as a communist work attitude in the best sense (ibid., p. 34), which may sound as strange to Western ears as his confessions to the Communist Party of China (cf. Plummer, 2018, pos. 3534 f.) and the special form of Maoist thinking at Huawei (cf. Tao, 2014, p. 62). In a somewhat less excited reading, this attitude can be understood to mean that Huawei is a decidedly Chinese company that cultivates cosmopolitanism in the manner of the ruling development of the CPC doctrine. For Ren Zhengfei, this statement also means not necessarily wanting to impose the Chinese view of things on international partners and employees, but to learn from them and use this knowledge for the ongoing development of their own culture:

"We must not force foreign employees to identify with the Chinese way. Perhaps we are not very clear about our own culture. In fact, Huawei's culture is like an onion with many layers; one layer is the British culture, another layer is Chinese, and still another is American. So I believe ours is an open and inclusive culture. We'd rather not ask them to follow the Chinese way, but use their gift with an open mind to enrich our culture." (Tao, 2014, p. 63).

Indeed, this remark is not only revealing for the myth of Huawei, but for the understanding of China in general. Ren speaks of a kind of *melting pot* at Huawei, which is by no means to be understood as a universalistic project in the pattern of the American Dream. The Chinese dream, on the other hand, refers specifically to the resurgence of the Chinese cultural nation in the demarcating coexistence with other cultures. Following the insight of *Deng Xiaoping*, however, it is important, regardless of all differences, to learn from the Western cultures perceived as progressive for one's own advancement: It is not so important whether a cat is black or white, as long as it catches mice. In this sense, Ren Zhengfei pursues a company philosophy described as *Huidu*—translated: grayness or shading—the aim of which is not to exclude any idea on the basis of ideological black-and-white thinking:

"Any absolute idea—be it black or white—can be very inspiring. But we don't need this. What we need is huidu. Maintaining a proper level of huidu—which means a balance of the grayness between black and white—is difficult, but that is what leaders and mentors should aspire to achieve." (Huang, 2018, pos. 3061).

However, openness, tolerance, and consideration of other ways of thinking are primarily intended as a guideline for the company's management, whose leadership style, however, follows the traditional Confucian Chinese model. It is therefore just as much the task of the CEO to shape the culture of the company with reference to the concept of Huidu as it is to manage the maintenance of the inner balance through strong steering (cf. Huang, 2018, pos. 518 ff.; Plummer, 2018, pos. 1094 ff.). Part of Huawei's corporate culture is therefore on the one hand to be open to new ideas and to promote the loyalty of employees to the company through participation in employee shares. On the other hand, Ren Zhengfei also carries out with strong will the measures he deems necessary, such as the dismissal and selective rehiring of thousands of employees. Such measures follow the same goal of promoting the inner balance and creative performance of the company as many years of high expenditure for management consulting by Western companies.

The success validates the growth strategy pursued here, with constant improvement of its own management and development competence. 25 years after its founding, Huawei became the world's largest manufacturer of telecommunications technology in 2012 (The Economist, 2012), and in the 2nd quarter of 2018, it became the second-largest manufacturer of smartphones, ahead of Apple and behind Samsung (Laricchia, 2023). With expenditures of $15.3 billion for Research and Development, Huawei claimed to be fourth worldwide in the same year, after Samsung and significantly ahead of Apple (Junior, 2019). Huawei's promise, it can be concluded, has been fulfilled in part by freeing itself from the role of the servant through its own efforts, just like the dream of a new China. Huawei thus represents a modern China, whose economy is capable of positioning its own innovative brands at the top of the global value chain.

With the election of *Donald Trump* as American president and the beginning of the trade war with China, the national origin of the brand has increasingly gained importance over its innovative power in international perception. In this regard, it can be initially noted that Huawei, like the Chinese manufacturer ZTE, was already portrayed as a threat to national security in a report by the House Intelligence Services in 2012 (see Plummer, 2018, pos. 2254 ff.). Although a relieving report was available in 2013, the company was subsequently unable to conclude distribution contracts with even one of the 4 relevant network operators in the USA. After the situation seemed to ease slightly through collaborations with *Google* and *Microsoft* in 2015/16, the dispute intensified considerably after the presidential election. Huawei is now being harshly attacked, particularly with regard to the upcoming establishment of the 5G network standard for mobile communications, as a threat to internal security. In addition, the brand's image in the American public worsens when *Meng Wanzhou*, daughter of Ren Zhengfei and CFO of the corporation, is publicly arrested in Canada in December 2018 at the request of the USA for an alleged violation of the US embargo against Iran. As a result, the share of Huawei smartphones as the primarily used smartphone in the USA drops to only 1% by 2019 (see Feldman, 2019). In May 2019, Trump then signs an executive order clearly aimed at Huawei to protect American telecommunications, which is followed in August 2019 by an explicit rejection of cooperation with Huawei at all levels (Wu, 2019). In response, Google, among other companies, also announces the termination of its cooperation with Huawei (see Weinstein, 2019). The manufacturer is thus not only excluded from services such as *Gmail* and the *Google Play Store* outside of China. More severe than this sanction is that Huawei is thereby denied the further development of the

Android operating system, which is vital for its smartphones even within China, in cooperation with Google. In August 2020, the US sanctions also hit its chip supplier, which can only produce the Kirin processor developed by Huawei using American technology, which now also falls under the ban imposed by the American government.

With the loss of the license for Google's operating system and the endangerment of the production of new innovative products, the brand is relegated from the role of the hero of the story back to the place of the underdog. Despite the high quality standard and cooperation with well-known brands such as *Porsche* and *Leica*, the brand could not maintain the worldwide leadership in smartphone sales beyond the 2nd quarter of 2020 (Laricchia, 2023). Also, the share of Huawei smartphone sales fell from 20% worldwide in the 2nd quarter to 8.4% in the 4th quarter of 2020 (ibid.). After this, the brand did not make it back into the top 5 of the largest smartphone manufacturers worldwide. However, during the same period, Huawei also achieved successes in the licensing business for 4G and 5G and made progress in integrating its own Google-Android alternative *Harmony OS* in the Internet of Things (IoT). Besides televisions and household appliances, the outstanding example of this is the integration of Huawei technology into electric cars from the manufacturer *Seres*, which was awarded with the *Huawei AITO M5* in 2023. There are also advances for cloud services and the reorientation towards new sales markets (ibid.). Since 2021, the Huawei brand has undergone a further development, in which it shifts its marketing strategy to long-term growth and brand building and invests heavily in R&D (Telecom Review, 2022). Despite the pandemic and US sanctions, the company finally recorded a return to growth, especially in its smartphone business, which recorded a growth of 41% in the first three months of 2023 after the introduction of a self-developed 5G chip in the flagship product (see Tomás, 2023).

Returning to Hegel in this context, one can recall his assumption that the internal logic of historical processes is not linear, but reflexive in advances and setbacks. The *cunning of reason* is always only recognizable in retrospect and often consists in achieving success despite or precisely because of opposing efforts. Sanctions and embargoes could, in this respect, prove to be disadvantageous in the short term, but decisive catalysts for new innovations in the long run. To what extent this will also apply to the technical further development of Huawei products in the future cannot yet be fully foreseen. The pressure to have to look for own solutions in chip manufacturing, as well as the continuous effort to be able to offer an alternative to Android with the operating system *Harmony*, points to the emerging era of a multipolar world also in the digital sector (cf. Plummer, 2018, pos. 14 ff.). Huawei will play a key role in a dispute that is increasingly becoming a question of the political system also with regard to different digital operating systems. It can finally be noted that the development so far has contributed to an international weakening of the brand, but Huawei is increasingly assuming the role of a national icon, which stands all the more for China's self-earned, conscious independence.

References

Arthur, C. (1983). *Hegel's master/slave dialectic and a myth of marxology*, In: New left review I/142 November–December 1983.
Body, P. (3 March 2023). Huawei or the highway. https://english.ckgsb.edu.cn/knowledges/huawei-or-the-highway/. Accessed 22 May 2023.
Campbell, J. (1949/2004). *The hero with a thousand faces.* Princeton University Press.
Fan, P. (2006). *Catching up through developing innovation capacity: Evidence from China's telecom equipment industry.* Technovation, 26, 359–368.
Feldman, S. (22 May 2019). Almost nobody in the U.S. Has a Huawei smartphone. https://www.statista.com/chart/18106/huawei-smartphone-use/. Accessed 20 Dec. 2023.
Fowke, E. F. (1973). *Songs of work and protest.* Dover Publications.
Huang, W. (2018). *Dedication: The foundations of Huawei's HR management* (kindle). LID Publishing.
Hegel, G. W. F. (1986). *Werke in 20 Bänden* (1st edn.). Suhrkamp. Vol. 7: Grundlinien der Philosophie des Rechts (Originalwerk veröffentlicht 1820).
Huawei Consumer BG. (22 December 2019). Huawei's annual smartphone shipments exceed 200 million units. https://consumer.huawei.com/en/press/news/2018/huawei-annual-smartphone-shipments-exceed-200-million-units/. Accessed 20 Dec. 2023.
Interbrand. (2023). Best global brands 2023 rankings. https://interbrand.com/best-global-brands/. Accessed 20 Dec. 2023.
Jacob, J. T., & Hoang, T. A. (2020). ‚National Rejuvenation' as Panacea for China's domestic and external challenges. In J. Jacob & Hoang, T. (Eds.), *China's search for ‚National Rejuvenation'*. Palgrave Macmillan. Accessed 20 Dec. 2023. https://doi.org/10.1007/978-981-15-2796-8_1.
Junior, J. H. (27 April 2019). Huawei's R&D budget reaches $15.3 billion, Outspends Apple. Huawei Central. https://www.huaweicentral.com/huaweis-rd-budget-reaches-15-3-billion-outspends-apple/. Accessed 30 Nov. 2023.

Kaufman, A. (2010). The 'century of humiliation', then and now: Changing Chinese perceptions of the international order. *Pacific Focus*, 25(1). https://doi.org/10.1111/j.1976-5118.2010.01039.x.

Laricchia. F. (8 November 2023). Quarterly smartphone market share worldwide by vendor 2009–2023. https://www.statista.com/statistics/271496/global-market-share-held-by-smartphone-vendors-since-4th-quarter-2009/. Accessed 20 Dec. 2023.

Nylander, J. (2017). *Shenzhen superstars – How China's smartest city is challenging Silicon Valley.* CreateSpace Independent Publishing Platform.

Plummer, W. D. (2018). *Huidu. Inside Huawei.* Kindle Edition.

Tao, T. (2014). *The Huawei story.* SAGE.

Tech.Ifeng.com. (1 December 2013). 任正非:华为名源自中华有为 我们要教外国人怎么念 (Ren Zhengfei: Der Name Huawei hat seinen Ursprung in „Zhonghua Youwei". Wir müssen den Ausländern beibringen, wie man es ausspricht). https://web.archive.org/web/20190603043947/http://tech.ifeng.com/telecom/detail_2013_12/01/31700411_0.shtml. Accessed 20 Dec. 2023.

Tuan Do. (7. Februar 2023). The Real Production Costs of Smartphone https://www.techwalls.com/production-costs-of-smartphones/. Accessed 20 Dec. 2023.

Telecom Review. (31 December 2022). Huawei shares detailed approach to reach its 2023 business goals. https://www.telecomreview.com/articles/telecom-vendors/6661-huawei-shares-detailed-approach-to-reach-its-2023-business-goals. Accessed 30 Nov. 2023.

The Economist. (4 August 2012). Who's Afraid of Huawei? https://www.economist.com/leaders/2012/08/04/whos-afraid-of-huawei. Accessed 20 Dec. 2023.

Tomás, J. P. (11 August 2023). Huawei returns to growth in H1 2023. *RCR Wireless News.* https://www.rcrwireless.com/20230811/network-infrastructure/huawei-returns-growth-h1-2023. Accessed 20 May 2023.

Weinstein, N. (20 May 2019). Google Cuts Off Huawei Phones from Future Android Updates. https://www.cnet.com/tech/mobile/google-reportedly-cuts-off-huawei-phones-from-future-android-updates/. Accessed 20 May 2023.

Wu, N. (15 May 2019). President Trump Signs Executive Order Potentially Banning Huawei Equipment. https://www.usatoday.com/story/news/politics/2019/05/15/trump-signs-executive-order-telecommunications-security-huawei/3685849002/. Accessed 18 May 2023.

4

Barack Obama: Back to the Future

Abstract Politics, especially in the United States, operates by the same standards as the marketing of products. A politician not only represents a specific brand of politics, but also stages himself as a brand, distinguishing himself in the fight for voter votes through conscious branding. In addition to positioning within the current political coordinate system, a special role is given to the view of history. In this regard, it is noticeable that not only Donald Trump, but also Barack Obama, communicatively sets a path into the future that begins in the past.

The most successful movie of 1985 revolves around the problem that any journey into the past would change the events that follow, which are then again in the future. Just as the time traveler *Marty McFly*, played by *Michael J. Fox* in his shining role, gets in his own way in *Robert Zemeckis'* comedy *Back to the Future* (1985) by sabotaging his parents' relationship before the moment of his own conception, time travel is always associated with risks for those venturing into the past. Unless they completely destroy the conditions of their own existence, the future influenced by them will deviate more or less strongly from the previous memory of their own past. With some luck, the time traveler, like Marty at the time, finds himself in an improved version of the present; however, only to find that this itself is again only the past of an imperfect future. In view of this, the time traveler is constantly doomed to straighten out the course of time, which in the case of the *Back to the Future franchise* has proven to be a lucrative endeavor.

As intellectually challenging and entertaining as our notions of time travelers may be, they will probably remain mere material for Hollywood films. Tourists from the future have never appeared in the present. Therefore, the working hypothesis seems permissible that at least the way back on the timeline will continue to be inaccessible to future generations. However, this does not mean that past events could not be changed in a way relevant for the future. We know the past only through the lens of subjective memories and based on emphases in historiography and other factors of public consciousness, which can be summarized under the broad term of *Zeitgeist*. In this sense, history is to be understood as a *symbolic form*, according to *Ernst Cassirer*, which, like religion or modern science, is responsible for the meaningful localization of man in his world (see Cassirer, 1923/2003). History is therefore significant in the present, and the present view of the past is always tied to the conditions of the present:

> "Historical knowledge is the answer to definite questions. An answer which must be given by the past; but the questions themselves are put and dictated by the present–by our present intellectual interests and our present moral and social needs." (Cassirer, 1944/1967, p. 178).

According to this understanding, every present has a specific interpretation of the past that is meaningful for it, from which the lines then extend again with a view to the future. Characteristic of the world of the past of 1955 and the future of 2015 visited by Marty McFly is therefore above all that the lines of historical image and vision of the future intersect from the perspective of the 1980s.

This connection between current expectations of the future and our perspective on the past is also addressed by Friedrich Nietzsche in his considerations *On the Use and Disadvantage of History for Life* (Nietzsche, KSA 1, p. 243 ff.) in 1874. He is concerned with more than just the mere observation that we know history only through the lens of the present. In this second piece of the *Untimely Meditations*, he advocates creatively reinterpreting history in a way that is beneficial for the future. In stark contrast to Cassirer's caution against fabricating mythical grand narratives (see Cassirer, 1944/1967, p. 179), history, according to Nietzsche's understanding, should be made fruitful as a myth for the present progressing into the future. On the way to this insight, he differentiates in his analyses between the perspectives of a *critical*, a *monumental*, and an *antiquarian* historiography. In this distinction, the monumental historian deals with glorious epochs and famous historical figures, which should encourage the recipient to perform similar deeds:

"He takes from it that the great, which was once there, was at least once possible and therefore will probably be possible again; he walks his path more courageously, for now the doubt that assails him in weaker hours, whether he might not want the impossible, is defeated." (Nietzsche, KSA 1, p. 265).

In contrast, the antiquarian view of history emphasizes the power of the community in a return to the tranquility of past times:

"Here it was possible to live, he tells himself, for it is possible to live, here it will be possible to live, for we are tough and not to be broken overnight. Thus he looks, with this 'we', beyond the transient, strange individual life and feels himself as the spirit of the house, the family, and the city." (Ibid.).

Nietzsche describes both modes against the background of a supposed crisis of society and its merely managing approach to history. He proposes as a cure for this "historical disease" (ibid., p. 332) of his time an artistic reinterpretation of history that primarily affects the youth. It is therefore a task for the creative power of man to shape an image of history in such a way that it is beneficial for the progression into the future.

It hardly requires further explanation that a forward-looking reference to history is of considerable importance, especially in the political events of Western democracies. Neither states nor individual parties or politicians can do without a version of history that is meaningful to them, on which they base their respective concept of the right politics. It is also not only a recent phenomenon that these concepts and the politicians associated with them become brands in the struggle for majorities. A certain *brand of politics* is ubiquitous, at least in the Anglo-American sphere. This has been the case not only since John F. Kennedy, New Labour, or Richard Nixon's first campaign, to which *Joe McGinnis* dedicated fundamental considerations on political marketing in *The Selling of the President 1968* (McGinnis, 1969). Anyone who remembers Latin lessons or Asterix comics and the words *ceterum censeo Carthaginem esse delendam* (cf. Kudla, 2007, p. 204) will have an idea that politics has always been accompanied by symbolic abbreviations of positions and exaggerations of personalities. This slogan not only indirectly contributed to the achievement of the political goal of destroying Carthage; the rhetorical figure of *Ceterum Censeo* also helped Cato the Elder (234–149 BC) to gain authority that has lasted for centuries. One could easily imagine election posters with a version of this slogan adapted to the present, on which Cato, with the high forehead of a Roman aristocrat, recommends himself as a principled and assertive candidate of a party.

Cato's trademark of constantly repeating a catchy phrase is still as effective a tool as it was in pre-Christian times. This pattern is evident today not only, but especially, in the so-called populist forces in politics. Apparently, a political campaign like the *Brexit* could only be successful because the message could be credibly reduced to five, actually three, words that could be repeated at every opportunity: "Vote leave, take back control" is the slogan of the party-independent Vote Leave Campaign Organization, which advocated leaving the EU during the Brexit vote (Vote Leave Campaign Organization, 2015). The abbreviation "take back control" encapsulates everything that is going wrong today, with the simple statement that the own population once held control in a past glorified into a comprehensive *Then*. In this sense, the strength of this slogan is mainly due to its relative indeterminacy. When, where, and how exactly the threads slipped can be flexibly adapted to the individual coordinate system of present disillusionment and past glorification.

More targeted than the Tories stumbling into EU exit, however, American politics in recent history has chosen a path back to the future. It can be said that both *Donald Trump* and *Barack Obama* have chosen Friedrich Nietzsche as their teacher. Nietzsche did not provide a precise guide for the artistic turn to history; but with the dichotomy of monumental and antiquarian history just introduced, he points to a progressive and a conservative center of gravity, in whose orbit the mythical glorification of one's own history can move at all. Affected by the gravity of traditionalism, the mythical consciousness asks how the former greatness of the past could be restored. Influenced by the attraction of progressive forces, however, the question dominates whether the heroic deeds of the past could not be accomplished again. In this sense, not only Donald Trump's 2016 campaign, which invokes the greatness of the past with the slogan "Make America Great again" borrowed from *Ronald Reagan*, but also Barack Obama's much more elaborate 2008 campaign follows the motif of a birth of the future from the spirit of the past.

The catchy slogan "Yes we can!" associated with this campaign does not yet contain strong historical implications when Obama first uses it in 2004 in a spot for his candidacy as Senator of Illinois. In this 30-second spot, he lists his and his party's successes in local politics in the contradictory style of a "they-said-it-was-impossible-but-we-did-it-anyway". The sequence ends with the statement that the apostrophized *Others* would *now* claim that Washington cannot be changed. According to a frequently recounted anecdote, Obama initially found his enthusiastic "Yes we can!" response to this stagnation "too corny"—a bit too flat (cf. Axelrodt, 2015, p. 142). The decision to stick with it is therefore solely due to his wife Michelle, which fits the image of the serious and highly educated Barack Obama, who is actually too cultured for professional branding, which necessarily involves catchy slogans and simplifications of complex contexts—and it fits the image of *Michelle Obama,* who here, as elsewhere, appears as the smart partner with a bit more sense of reality than her husband, who tends to intellectual aloofness.

For the Obama brand, it is just as essential as for any other brand that the artificiality recedes behind the impression of authenticity. Although, or rather: because this is probably the most uncompromising branding of a president to date (cf. Zavattaro, 2010), the necessary abbreviations and exaggerations for a brand should recede behind the public person Obama presented as authentic. In fact, it is one of these simplifications that already gives the commercial for the Senate seat in Illinois a touch of the historical. Thus, in the first five seconds of his advertisement, Obama does not speak about politics at all, but about the fact that he took over the leadership of the *Harvard Law Review* in 1990 because no African American had ever been at its head: "They said, an African American has never led the Harvard Law Review, that's why I changed that." (Obama for Senate, 2004).

This statement is as indispensable for Obama's *brand of politics* as it must astonish upon closer examination. It is astonishing that historical justice for African Americans, and not professional ambitions and merits, should have been the reason for taking on this honorable task. At the same time, it is noticeable that this first statement has not been formulated contradictorily, although such a choice of words would have fit much better into the rhythm of the spot. So Obama does not say, "They said, an African American cannot lead the Harvard Law Review," but makes the factual statement that no African American has succeeded in this position before him. The reason for this weaker formulation is probably that, unlike many other institutions in the USA, there was no common prejudice among the elite of American lawyers in the early 1990s about the impossibility of an African American in this position. However, in the context of the following statements about the refutation of prejudices, the opening statement suggests this assumption. The spot thus suggests a version of the past that fits better into the message because the candidate was ready to overcome all institutional hurdles that existed for African Americans up to that point.

The newly elected Senator from Illinois already shares this journey with the broad American public in July 2004. Thus, his keynote at the National Convention of the Democratic Party begins with the remark that the appearance of the son of a Kenyan immigrant on this stage is quite unlikely:

"Let's face it, my presence on this stage is pretty unlikely." (Reid, 2017, p. 6). This typical Obama, humorous opening statement serves as a self-ironic icebreaker that sets the theme of the entire speech. The strength of the subsequent elaborations then lies in understanding this own success as an example of the ongoing success of the American project. After well-chosen words about individual opportunities, the unity of the nation beyond party lines, personal experiences in encounters with the population, and repeated references to the presidential candidate *John Kerry*, Obama finally sharpens his speech to hope as the leitmotif of belief in this progress:

> "It's the hope of slaves sitting around a fire singing freedom songs; the hope of immigrants setting out for distant shores; the hope of a young naval lieutenant bravely patrolling the Mekong Delta; the hope of a millworker's son who dares to defy the odds; the hope of a skinny kid with a funny name who believes that America has a place for him, too." (Barack Obama, quoted after Dionne & Reid, 2017, p. 12).

With this second humorous self-comment, with which Obama brings the arc back to the opening statement, he shows himself ostensibly humble towards this unique nation. Only in America could this now not so small lanky boy with the funny name find his place in life. Not *only* humility, however, is evidenced at the same moment by bringing into play, *en passant*, the question of whether hope and progress will carry the speaker himself to the top of the state, on the occasion of the inauguration party of another candidate before a national audience. After all, Obama has made it to Senator of Illinois and keynote speaker at the Democratic Convention. The trick performed here is not only that he successfully positions himself as the future hope of the party without appearing too ambitious. It also lies in the short circuit of history and biography, successfully stylizing his own aspirations as the hope of the entire country.

In the design of the corporate identity for the 2008 presidential campaign, this motif was condensed, with Obama using the keywords "Hope" and "Change" to invite participation in this hero's journey. The logo already stands out from everything that has come before in that it is more reminiscent of a company's signet than that of an American campaigner (cf. Arnon, 2017). Too "corporate" as Obama himself is said to have noted (Axelrodt, 2015, p. 209); perhaps also to distract from how professionally he approached the issue of his own branding. Iconographically, the logo initially reminds of a whole series of generic logos, in which agricultural areas and blue sky are arranged in a circle in such a way that the paths or furrows lead from the foreground to the horizon line. One can easily imagine this type of logo on the baseball cap of a farmer in Illinois, which also gives Obama's branding a certain degree of down-to-earthness. The circle stands equally for the sky and rising sun as well as for the name Obama, the red and white stripes symbolize both the American flag and furrows and in their dynamic swing from left to right the way forward, this logo is an example of the condensation of several levels of meaning in a simple sign (Lidwell et al., 2003, p. 190 f.). It remains to be seen whether a certain *proposition density* (ibid., p. 191) of this logo can be determined, which can provide meaningful information about the success of a logo. However, it is true that it is not only taken up as a logo for this campaign, but also as an authentic symbol for the societal awakening in pop culture.

A significant contribution to this is made by a series of works by the street artist *Shepard Fairey*, who has been interested in Obama's political career since the 2004 party convention speech. In the works created in 2008, Fairey takes advantage of a return to history by designing his artworks "Obama Hope", "Obama Change" and "Obey Progress" after the model of socialist revolution posters (Fairey, 2009, p. 270 ff.). In addition, the Obama portrayed in the portrait with a slight low angle view looking upwards reminds of iconic shots of *Che Guevara* or *Martin Luther King*. Obama, so the message of this poster series, can connect with his politics to the societal awakening of the 1960s in the United States. Remarkable about the 3000 posters put up by Fairey himself without the campaign office's order in public space at the beginning of 2008 is that these, unlike the edition of 350 posters sold out in no time in his online shop, carry the unchanged logo of the Obama campaign. The sign is thus somewhat removed from the context of the election campaign and, through the literal *street credibility* of the artist, becomes an authentic symbol of a citizens' movement leaning to the left of the center, connecting to the progressive spirit of the 1960s. The resulting image of Obama as a hopeful renewer with revolutionary claim also carries on for quite a while after his election to the presidency, to which the reprocessed version of the Hope poster, which appears on the cover of the *TIME Magazine* at the end of 2008, declaring the newly elected president man of the year, also contributes (cf. Stengel, 2008).

However, Obama receives artistic tailwind not only through this congenial collaboration with Shepard Fairey, but with an even greater reach through the pop song "Yes we can", which is released in February 2008 (will.i.am., 2008). Here too, it is not a release coordinated with the election campaign, but a self-production of the artist *William James Adams Jr.*, known under the stage name *will.i.am*, created in collaboration with many famous stars of the entertainment industry. Noteworthy is not only the unique circumstance that both the words of a victory speech and the slogan of an ongoing primary campaign are processed in an independent and quite popular pop anthem. It is also remarkable that Obama gives this speech prepared for the event of victory despite the defeat against *Hillary Clinton* in the New Hampshire primaries. This circumstance makes the historical mission invoked by pop artists of the liberal elite appear even more urgent, which Obama understands as a continuation of the narrative of America as the promised land:

> "It was a creed written into the founding documents that declared the destiny of a nation. Yes we can. It was whispered by slaves and abolitionists as they blazed a trail towards freedom through the darkest of nights. Yes we can. It was sung by immigrants as they struck out from distant shores and pioneers who pushed westward against an unforgiving wilderness. Yes we can. It was the call of workers who organized; women who reached for the ballot; a President who chose the moon as our new frontier; and a King who took us to the mountaintop and pointed the way to the Promised Land. Yes we can to justice and equality. Yes we can to opportunity and prosperity. Yes we can heal this nation. Yes we can repair this world. Yes we can." (Barack Obama, quoted after Dionne & Reid, 2017, p. 49).

The career of the slogan *Yes we can!*, initially perceived as too intrusive, from a rather ordinary election advertisement to the most American of all creeds, is also reflected in the pathos with which Obama emphasizes the missionary mandate of his campaign by referring to *Abraham Lincoln*. Already in 2004, he introduced himself at the party convention as the senator from Illinois, the "Land of Lincoln", and announced his intended candidacy for the presidential election campaign in adverse weather on the market square in Lincoln's hometown of Springfield. As an elected president, he embarks on his journey by train to Washington just like his predecessor from Illinois—and finally takes his oath of office on Abraham Lincoln's Bible.

In the construction of the political brand Obama, it can be observed that all the good spirits from America's history were successfully invoked and the young president was already glorified as a mythical hero figure upon taking office. Nothing illustrates this resounding success better than the nomination for the Nobel Peace Prize within the first two weeks of his term, which Obama is awarded in September and which he then receives in December 2009. This prize, awarded by the committee for Obama's *vision of a better world* (The Nobel Foundation, 2009) and thus on the credit of deeds yet to be accomplished, primarily shows the height from which Obama begins his presidency. However, it is already doubtful at the time of receiving this highest award for social commitment whether the global euphoria about his election will also result in a historic presidency.

However one may evaluate the years of the Obama administration in retrospect, the insight remains that the political day-to-day business cannot live up to the invoked myths of the past *can*. Certainly, such a contrast between narrative and reality of life can be found in every brand. It is also worth noting that the American election campaign is always a bit more bombastic and the person is much more in the center than in Europe, for example. However, Obama not only advanced the professionalization of political branding, but also a nearly messianic expectation of the office.

A successor who also made it into office as a political outsider through his version of a historically attested better America could build on these prerequisites. The reference to the emancipatory movements as a resource for a successful election campaign has probably exhausted itself with the end of the Obama era. However, the mythologizing view of supposedly better times seems to be just gaining momentum at the same moment. "Yes we can… make America great again" can be grammatically correctly continued from Obama's slogan, with which *Jordi* Graupera (2016) critically points out parallels between Obama and Trump. Following this reading, Donald Trump's branding is to be understood as a shift from a *monumental* history to an *antiquarian* version of history that draws its strength from the resentment of the *we* against the *others*. In this context, a parallel between Barack Obama and Marty McFly is not entirely far-fetched, who in the sequel *Back to the Future Part II* (Zemeckis, 1989) has to experience the abuse of the time machine by his arch-enemy *Biff Tannen*. This character, probably inspired by Donald Trump (Collins, 2017), shows that the technique of time travel, if it falls into the wrong hands, can lead to terrible consequences. This statement also applies to the technique of creating a political myth, which both Barack Obama in 2008 and Donald Trump in 2016 used.

Under the impression of the devastations of National Socialism, Ernst Cassirer rejects this fabricated political myth as an evil technique *sui generis*, which he considers a means suitable only in totalitarian states for seducing and paralyzing the masses (Cassirer, 1946/2009, p. 281 ff.). Cassirer differentiates in his argumentation between the natural myths of the past and the technically fabricated political myth of the 20th century:

> "Myth has always been described as the result of an unconscious activity and as a free product of imagination. But here we find myth made according to

plan. The new political myths do not grow up freely; they are not wild fruits of an exuberant imagination." (Cassirer, 1946/2009, p. 277).

These explanations also clarify what exactly he means by the term *unconscious fiction* (Cassirer, 1944/1967, p. 74) mentioned elsewhere, which gives validity to the myths of the past. It is based on the assumption that traditional myths are not attributable to the purposes of a specific person, party, or brand, but have developed over generations in an activity of the general consciousness that is unconscious to the individual. As individuals each exist in their own time, they cannot easily become aware of human imagination as the origin of the myth that arose long before their time and the rites associated with it. Instead, the individual who believes in the myth behaves and feels towards the mythical narrative as if it were a truth that has always been valid. In contrast, the newly created political myths of the 20th century have neither a long tradition nor are they free from specific purposes in their genesis. On the contrary, they are the products of a purpose-rational technique that can be used as a weapon in the battle for minds: "Henceforth myths can be manufactured in the same sense and according to the same methods as any other modern weapon—as machine guns or airplanes." (Cassirer, 1946/2009, p. 277).

In view of the enormous impact of fascist propaganda, Cassirer sees little chance of refuting mythical thinking *in situ* with arguments—once a myth is emotionally anchored, it becomes virtually immune to rational objections (ibid.). Therefore, science must start earlier and examine the political myth in order to combat it through enlightenment about its structure right from its beginnings:

> "We should carefully study the origin, the structure, the methods, and the technique of the political myths. We should see the adversary face to face in order to know how to combat him." (Cassirer, 1946/2009, p. 291).

It is worth considering that in describing the myth fabricated by the National Socialists, he asserts those features that we have already encountered in dealing with the myths of brands. Here too, it is about identification with symbols and associated narratives that appeal to people in an emotional way. To Cassirer's realization that the mythically colored neologisms in the rallies of the National Socialists were created by masters of political propaganda (ibid., p. 280), it must finally be added that the same mastery also applies to many designers, artists, architects, event organizers, filmmakers, and many others involved.

It may initially sound trivializing to apply the professionalization of modern terms such as branding, corporate design, corporate architecture, corporate behavior, event planning, or even corporate culture to the self-presentation of the National Socialists (cf. Koop, 2012). Conversely, the reference to the structural equality of design means in Nazi dictatorship and market economy is important in order not to trivialize the dangers associated with the possibilities of holistic brand building. This assessment is all the more valid because Cassirer's hope for a complete overcoming of the political myth remained unfulfilled. Given political campaigns with good intentions and the task of inspiring many people for political goals, it is questionable whether the technical fabrication of the modern political myth is reason enough to fundamentally reject it in political events. From this perspective, one could agree with *Herfried Mückler* that a high degree of political participation also demands a high presence of mythical grand narratives (cf. Münckler, 2010, p. 490). Nevertheless, recent developments give cause for concern and make us aware of the responsibility that extends beyond the political message to the techniques of its transmission.

References

Arnon, B. (2017). Politics meets brand design: The story of Obama's campaign logo. https://www.huffpost.com/entry/politics-meets-brand-desi_b_151317. Accessed 20 Dec. 2023.
Axelrod, D. (2015). *Believer: My forty years in politics*. Penguin.
Cassirer, E. (2003). *Aufsätze und kleine Schriften (1922–1926)*. Meiner Verlag (ECW 16), darin: Der Begriff der symbolischen Form im Aufbau der Geisteswissenschaften (Originalwerk veröffentlicht 1923).
Cassirer, E. (1967). *An Essay on Man: An introduction to a philosophy of human culture*. Yale University Press. (Originalwerk veröffentlicht 1944).
Cassirer, E. (2009). *Gesammelte Werke*, Hrsg. von Birgit Recki. Bd. 25 (ECW 25). Meiner Verlag. Darin: The Myth of the State. (Originalwerk veröffentlicht 1946).
Collins, B. (2015/2017). ‚Back to the future' writer: Biff Tannen is based on Donald Trump. https://www.thedailybeast.com/back-to-the-future-writer-biff-tannen-is-based-on-donald-trump. Accessed 20 Dec. 2023.
Dionne, E. J., Jr., & Reid, J.-A. (Eds.). (2017). We are the change we seek: The speeches of Barack Obama. Bloomsbury USA.
Fairey, S. (2009). *Supply and demand: The works of Shepard Fairey*. Ginko Press Inc.
Gehlen, A. (1993). *Der Mensch. Seine Natur und seine Stellung in der Welt*. In ders. Gesamtausgabe, Bd. 3.1, herausgegeben von K.-S. Rehberg.. Vittorio Klostermann (Originalwerk veröffentlicht 1950).

Graupera, J. (2016). Yes, we can make America great again'. https://www.ara.cat/opinio/Jordi-Graupera-yes-we-can-make-America-great-again_0_1711028915.html. Accessed 20 Dec. 2023.

Kudla, H. (2007). *Lexikon der lateinischen Zitate*. C.H. Beck.

Koop, A. (2012). *NSCI- Das visuelle Erscheinungsbild der Nationalsozialisten 1920–1945*. Verlag Hermann Schmidt.

Lidwell, J., Holden, K., & Butler, W. (2003). *Universal principles of design*. Rockport Publishers.

McGinnis, J. (1969). *The selling of the president 1968*. Trident Press (Simon & Schuster).

Münkler, H. (2010). *Die Deutschen und ihre Mythen*. Rowohlt Verlag.

Obama for Senate. (2004). Ad „Yes We Can". https://www.youtube.com/watch?v=wqrm1_X-DsQ. Accessed 20 Dec. 2023.

Stengel, R. (2008). Person of the Year 2008: Why we Chose Obama. http://content.time.com/time/specials/packages/article/0,28804,1861543_1865068_1867014,00.html. Accessed 20 Dec. 2023.

The Nobel Foundation. (2009). The Nobel Peace Prize for 2009. https://www.nobelprize.org/prizes/peace/2009/press-release/. Accessed 20 Dec. 2023.

Vote Leave Campaign Organization. (2015). Why Vote Leave. http://www.voteleavetakecontrol.org/. Accessed 10 Jan. 2024.

Person of the Year 2008: Why we Chose Obama will.i.am (2008). *Yes We Can*. Will.i.am Music Group.

Zavattaro, S. (2010). Brand Obama: The implications of a branded president. *Administrative Theory & Praxis.*, *32*, 123–128. https://doi.org/10.2753/ATP1084-1806320108.

Zemeckis, R. (1985). *Back to the future*. Universal Pictures.

Zemeckis, R. (1989). *Back to the future Part II*. Universal Pictures.

5

Fridays For Future: Genuine Authenticity

Abstract Authenticity plays a prominent role in our self-understanding, in the perception of other people, and also in brand personalities. Contrary to the idea, however, that one simply has to be oneself, it is not easy to say when exactly one is truly authentic beyond all practiced roles. Looking at a personality considered authentic like Greta Thunberg, who stands for the movement Fridays For Future, which can indeed be understood as a brand, the question arises to what extent the professional staging of a brand excludes any authenticity or, conversely, is to be understood as its condition.

The self-expectation of a person and the societal expectation of them probably diverge nowhere as much as in the question regularly posed to adolescents about what they intend to "become" later. Indeed, this question is already somewhat treacherous because young people are always already something—namely themselves. Western philosophy has, at the latest since Heraclitus, drawn the conclusion that no specific profession, but the self yet to be explored, is worth all efforts in life. Friedrich Nietzsche then encapsulates this insight centuries later in a catchy formula: "Become who you are!" (Nietzsche, KSA 4, p. 297).

In the first half of the 20th century, this self-becoming and, even more, its regular failure is one of the main motifs of existential philosophy. Thus, *Martin Heidegger* presents in *Being and Time* (1927/1967) a phenomenology of the inauthentic "They" that describes the impossibility of individual self-becoming due to the integration of the individual human being, the "Dasein," as he expresses it, into society:

"This being-together dissolves the own Dasein completely into the mode of being 'of the others', in such a way that the others in their distinctness and expressiveness disappear even more. In this inconspicuousness and non-determinability, 'the They' unfolds its actual dictatorship. We enjoy and amuse ourselves as one enjoys; we read, see and judge literature and art as one sees and judges; we also withdraw from the 'great crowd' as one withdraws; we find 'outrageous' what one finds outrageous. 'The They', which is not a specific one and which all, though not as a sum, are, prescribes the mode of being of everydayness." (Heidegger, 1927/1967, p. 126f.)

Also, *Jean Paul Sartre* holds a similar view and develops in his main work *Being and Nothingness*(Sartre, 1943/1991) the motif of *insincerity towards oneself* (ibid., p. 132 ff.). Sartre describes a state in which people often, due to their social role, are not able to find their actual being. Sartre finds their mode of "being that which I am not" (ibid., p. 141) insincere because people deceive themselves that their actual self coincides with their role in society. The most famous example of this inversion is the café waiter who is prevented from being himself by his role as the waiter – a role that is completely foreign to him:

"No matter how much I may fulfill the function of a waiter, I can only be it in a neutralized way, just as the actor is Hamlet, by mechanically making the typical movements of my profession and looking at myself as an imaginary waiter over these movements taken as an analogue." (ibid., p. 142).

Therefore, no one is really a waiter, greengrocer, farmer, or policeman—and anyone who confuses these roles with their actual self is nothing less than insincere towards themselves. Obviously, Sartre assumes that this fundamental failure necessarily occurs in waiters, but not in philosophy professors, which can certainly be accused of some arrogance towards other milieus. Besides this *déformation professionnelle*, typical for professional thinkers, it is also difficult to understand where the real self is to be found outside of all involvement in activities in the world. A waiter is not always a waiter, even if Sartre suggests it, but also as a friend, husband, bachelor, lover, subtenant or even as an existentialist, he is always also determined by his role in exchange with others.

Following a critique of the overuse of the thought figure of supposedly sincere actual being, *Theodor W. Adorno* speaks critically in the 1960s, largely in distinction to Heidegger, of a *Jargon of Authenticity* (Adorno, 1970), which many of his contemporaries carried in their mouths. In this, he recognizes a hubris of being chosen, as already shines through with Sartre. Thus, these colleagues seem to have an authentic, actual life beyond all roles not only possible but also already realized in their own life design. With this assumption, however, they are not at the actual self, but only at a role clearly defined in the intellectual scene. Adorno skewers this circumstance with the malicious remark that one of his friends has experienced rejection from this intellectual circle because he was not able to meet their cliché of authenticity: "He was, as they told him, not authentic enough." (Ibid., p. 2825).

Although these explanations clearly show that the actual self must prove to be a problematic concept upon not too much reflection, the idea of a desirable authentic being beyond the everyday is a fixed part of modern life. Self-realization in leisure and work is increasingly given high importance, which seems to be impressively proven by the permanently booming industry of coaches and self-discovery trainers. However, this increase does not necessarily have to speak for the possibility of a successful self-search. Rather, this search could result in a need for *relief* from the disappointment that in the post-heroic age of division of labor, any activity could potentially be taken over by another. The possibly associated feeling of powerlessness and insignificance therefore seems to be overcome only by reflecting on an actual, everyday hustle and bustle hidden *self*. The mythical place of longing untouched by civilization, *Arcadia*, into which the Renaissance dreamed itself, shifts with the assumption that beyond everyday demands, a completely different, *truly authentic self* can be found.

This longing finds its expression, for example, in the comic character *Superman*, invented in 1938 by *Jerry Siegel* and *Joe Shuster*. In his dual identity as an average guy and superhuman, unlike normal existences, he is able to fully live out all the potentials of his actual self. This character shows that the idea of the actual self only works in a dual nature against the backdrop of everyday being. Without this part of normal existence, Superman would appear one-dimensional, and *Clark Kent* would be just a conformist without self-realization as Superman. Considering this, it is not a foregone conclusion which of these identities reveals the actual authentic self. It seems more convincing that both roles only gain authenticity in combination with the other.

The great attraction that emanates from this and from the myth of authenticity in general is also evident in the fact that the narrative pattern of the superhero has found countless imitators in a modified form. It seems no coincidence that parallel to the self-discovery industry, superhero films have gained enormous popularity in their endless sequels and remakes in recent decades. With *Todd Philips*'film *Joker* (2019), the super villain as the actual superhero has finally arrived in the mainstream. One can also go a step further and say that this character finds its real incarnation in the role of an American president, who impresses with nothing so much as authenticity that breaks all norms. The doubling of the actual roles described above is evident in the fact that *Donald Trump* is actually a figure from show business who has quite literally taken on the role of the American president. The key to the success of the 45th president may therefore lie in the fact that his supporters did not elect a politician, but a figure from their world of life, who as a superhero in the role of the statesman lives out all the extravagances denied to themselves (see Brown, 2016).

Indeed, it is this mechanism of borrowed self-realization that is also responsible for the success of brand personalities. Brands reflect personality attributes onto consumers as they would like to find them in themselves. One can say that the durability of certain brand personalities, as *David Aaker* describes it, lies in this interaction:

> "For example, one analysis found Coke to be considered real and authentic whereas Pepsi was young, spirited, and exciting and Dr. Pepper was nonconforming, unique, and fun. Further, the personalities of all three brands had endured over time, sometimes in efforts and augment to change them." (Aaker, 1996, p. 142).

This durability of the consumer's relationship to the actual authentic core of a brand is particularly evident in the fact that brands and their myths work independently of certain products or product classes (see Gerken, 1994, p. 204 ff.; Meffert et al., 2002, p. 27 ff.). The strength of the *fractal brand* in this way is that its respective myth can be the bracket for many different product categories. With the cigarette brand Camel, for example, clothing can also be marketed very well, because customers are concerned with the certain character traits associated with the brand and conveyed by the narratives, which they themselves would actually like to live out if everyday life allowed them the necessary freedom.

This and other examples also show that authenticity for brands is not problematic in the same way as for people. Unlike flesh-and-blood personalities, brands do not take on everyday roles that would distract them from this actual self. On the contrary, this inner part turns outward in them, as they are the projection surfaces of an ideal *self*, the authenticity in its pure form. However, this reveals the opposite problem, that brands lack the approachability that flesh-and-blood people have in their everyday dealings with other people. Brands are, one could say, constantly Superman and therefore have to actively strive for the role of Clark Kent.

Sponsorships, events, testimonials, and brand ambassadors can be understood as the classic means for brands to get a bit closer to this authentic everyday life. For these occasions, celebrities are often used, people who themselves have already assumed the status of a brand. Thus, testimonials from athletes, actors, and pop stars are forms of co-branding, where one brand lends a piece of its authenticity to the other. Although these are sometimes very successful collaborations, it remains questionable to what extent the gap between everyday life and brand can actually be closed with this. Not only does it seem unbelievable in many cases when a famous face advertises a certain product. In addition, the task of the cooperation is not always to create a closeness to the brand. For example, when a top tennis player like *Roger Federer* switches from *Nike* to *Uniqlo*, this $300 million takeover (cf. Rovell, 2018) shows more the strength of the textile giant from the Far East against its American competitor than it brings the brand closer to us on a human level.

In the age of social media, this problem seems to be solved by *influencer marketing* taking up an increasingly large space in product advertising. By broadcasting the life of a normal person to the consumer's smartphone, two problems seem to be solved at once. On the one hand, the brand gains that authenticity that arises from the everyday use of the products in everyday situations. At the same time, consumers can be addressed more directly with influencers taken from the context of the respective target group. As rapidly as influencer marketing has developed in recent years, so too has its professionalization progressed. The internet celebrities are now a class of their own, whose everyday life has little to do with that of their followers. The supposedly unobstructed view of the everyday activities of normal people has thus transparently become a staging like any other commercial.

If one were looking for an example of a truly authentic hero and influencer beyond the mass-produced stars of internet marketing, one would find it in the environmental movement *Fridays For Future* and its iconic founding figure *Greta Thunberg*. It is obvious that her position stems primarily from the fact that she credibly plays not just a role. Her authentic attitude makes her the conscience and face of this movement, and she embodies the myth of authenticity in several respects. This observation primarily applies to her youthful age and comparatively childlike demeanor, which seems to protect her from the intrusions of Heidegger's *They*: She has not yet become what *one* becomes. At the same time, however, she is attributed a mental maturity that surpasses adults. Views and demands that would probably be interpreted as naive, undercomplex, and well-known in the case of other teenagers appear in her case as expressions of great insight and seriousness.

This perception is further substantiated by the Asperger's syndrome diagnosed in her, which gives her a special position even among her peers. Greta may not come from the planet Krypton, but she too was given a superpower:

> "I have Asperger's and that means I'm sometimes a bit different from the norm. And—given the right circumstances—being different is a superpower. #aspiepower." (Greta Thunberg, quoted after Limburg, 2019).

Although she does not have a particular savant skill, she can tie in with the ideas about the special intellectual abilities of people on the autism spectrum that have been popular at least since *Barry Levinson's* film *Rain Man* (1988). Thus, the idea of autism as an actual strength is also associated with *Elon Musk*, who in turn is an outstanding example of an authentic influencer personality at the core of a brand (cf. Isaacson, 2023, p. 165).

In contrast to macho figures like Musk, it is not insignificant for Greta Thunberg that we are dealing with a *Super-Girl*. Crucial for this is that the problem of man-made climate change is considered to be caused mainly by men, not only among feminists. The fact that *one*, in the sense of the gender contained in this pronoun, is responsible for climate change, makes it plausible that it is now up to *woman* to take the right path here as elsewhere. In addition, she is assigned to female role models, as the sometimes spiteful Thunberg internet memes as Virgin Mary, Joan of Arc or Sophie Scholl prove. In a positive sense, she also has the spiritual purity of these figures, as claimed by the magazine *The New Yorker* for Greta Thunberg (cf. Kormann, 2019).

Finally, their nationality also plays a role not to be underestimated. Scandinavia is a place of longing for many, its image standing for a high degree of social care, ecological awareness, and progressive lifestyle. This image is further rounded off by the many child heroes of the children's book author *Astrid Lindgren*. Indeed, the story of the little girl who demonstrates every Friday in front of the Swedish Parliament for attention in connection with the impending climate change sounds like a tale from Lindgren. Greta Thunberg appears as defiant as *Lotta*, as strong as *Pippi Longstocking* and perhaps a bit peculiar like *Karlsson on the Roof*. Like these characters from Lindgren's children's books, Greta Thunberg credibly stands for the fact that the realities of children's lives are relevant and must be taken seriously by the overpowering adults. Certainly, the great Swedish author knew nothing of social media and the possibilities of information dissemination via the internet; but her story would probably also have the punchline that the little girl, with the help of the other children, manages to expose the adults' indifference to an urgent problem.

However, it should be added as a caveat that she would not have fit into one of Astrid Lindgren's stories in the role of *Cassandra,* who wants to panic the world of adults above all (cf. Vagianos, 2019). Where Lindgren is more concerned with a balance between generations, the narrative of Greta follows an irreconcilable contrast between childlike authenticity on the one hand and the failure of adults in the role of insincere inauthenticity on the other. On the cover pages of leading magazines or on conference panels, she conveys the corresponding image of the teenager with a problem awareness that has been lost to adults in everyday *business as usual.* This attitude reaches a climax in the angry *How dare you-refrain* of her speech at the UN Climate Summit 2019:

> "This is all wrong. I shouldn't be standing here. I should be back in school on the other side of the ocean. Yet you all come to us young people for hope? How dare you! You have taken away my dreams and my childhood with your empty words. And yet I'm one of the lucky ones. People are suffering. People are dying. Entire ecosystems are collapsing. We are in the beginning of a mass extinction. And all you can talk about is money and fairy tales of eternal economic growth. How dare you!" (Thunberg, 2019, p. 96).

At this moment, however, she appears not only defiant and witty, but also stubborn and strangely detached. Accordingly, she probably generated a lot of positive resonance with her supporters with this statement; but there are also numerous internet memes reacting to this outburst, which strongly criticize and ridicule Greta Thunberg. The rejection suggests that with this performance she has already exceeded the furthest point of how she can convey her message without being perceived as mentally out of role. However, even in this performance, she respects a boundary of the sayable, which lies between pointing out grievances and concrete proposals. Since Greta Thunberg has put her followers in a predicament with a positive statement about nuclear power (cf. Kessler, 2019), she seems to actually refrain from making her own very specific contributions to solutions against climate change. She does not have to understand this as her task in her role. Greta Thunberg and the brand Fridays For Future stand more for the authentic and justified demand of young people that the adults responsible for climate damage rethink and take measures to achieve the 1.5-degree target (cf. Fridays For Future, 2023).

The designation as a brand does not have to be in quotation marks here, not only because Greta Thunberg is seeking to register Fridays for Future and her own name as brands at the beginning of 2020 (cf. The Guardian, 2020). Even if this is not a commercial organization with a strategy for its own brand appearance, the ritualization of the strikes and their export to the whole world has established the clearly recognizable global brand Fridays for Future. In this sense, one can speak of a *natural brand formation* here, which is not the product of a conscious effort, and which needs to be protected from third-party access by trademark law (cf. Domizlaff, 1939/2005, p. 183).

The reference to the organic-natural growth of the brand *outside of the conscious awareness* of Greta Thunberg, who herself has expressed her actual disinterest in branding (cf. The Guardian, 2020), could also be too naive. In fact, given the rapid media success of *Fridays For Future* and the presence of Greta Thunberg, it is not far-fetched to assume that her story is based on a script trained in Swedish children's literature. The photos of her early protest in front of the Swedish parliament, suitable for exploitation before a broad audience, could point in the direction of a systematic build-up of the public persona Greta Thunberg, as insinuated by critics. If authenticity means the unobstructed access to a person's true self beyond all societal involvement and the strategic considerations associated with it, then this would indeed be fatal for the credibility of the brand. However, the discussion of authenticity reveals how problematic this concept is as such. More sensible, on the other hand, is the question of whether knowledge of professional staging harms our impression of authenticity. If one considers authenticity not as an ontological, but as an aesthetic category, this does not necessarily have to be damaging. According to this interpretation, the question of authenticity is not about authenticity in the strict, indeed *actual* sense, but about whether the *representation of the authentic* is meaningful to the viewer.

Such a shift in perspective is known, for example, from visual art and criticism of naive realism. The idea that images can simply copy the actual reality has given way here to the insight that every image is mediated by the perspective of the artist on the one hand and its reception on the other. An impressionistic painting created in nature is therefore not less, but also not necessarily more authentic than classical studio painting or high-resolution contemporary landscape photography. It depends on whether the subject is authentically represented. Similarly, the story of a novel character is not necessarily less authentic than a report of an experience. Rather, it is often the case that the technique of storytelling can bring certain situations much closer in their complexity than the less elaborated reports of contemporary witnesses can achieve. Also, the fact that the actor on stage is not really Hamlet, we can understand as the condition for the *authentic*reproduction of an inner conflict that living people probably feel, but cannot convey as an artist can in his play. According to this interpretation, it is obvious that Greta Thunberg was only able to authentically convey the urgency of the climate problem thanks to very professional support in telling her story and thus building her myth. We must understand the will to self-presentation and conscious brand building here as well as elsewhere not in opposition, but as an integral part of authenticity. Therefore, it would not at all speak against her authenticity if the environmental activist Greta Thunberg had consciously decided to present in public what *They* imagine a dedicated young environmentalist to be in the best sense.

Since the image of authenticity of a still becoming person wears off particularly quickly, it is by no means certain whether the hearts can be won over in the long term with the young climate activist. At the beginning of the 2020s, Greta Thunberg still ideally represents the protest of those who did not actually cause climate change themselves. Now in her twenties, however, she already belongs to the establishment of an environmental movement, which is increasingly associated with the image of bourgeois satiety in contrast to the activism of newer movements. At the same time, the problems of aligning a brand with a person who always behaves authentically in her own way are reflected in the irritations that her statements, which do not directly concern climate policy, also cause at Fridays For Future.

References

Aaker, D. A. (1996). *Building strong brands.* Free Press.
Adorno, T. W. (1970). *Negative Dialektik. Jargon der Eigentlichkeit* (Gesammelte Werke vol. 6). Suhrkamp Verlag.
Brown, T. K. (10. June 2016). Why they love Trump: 'He's not a politician'. https://www.bbc.com/news/av/election-us-2016-36493676/why-they-love-trump-he-s-not-a-politician. Accessed 20 Dec. 2023.
Boxoffice Mojo. (April 2020). Top Lifetime Grosses. https://www.boxofficemojo.com/chart/top_lifetime_gross/?area=XWW. Accessed 29 Apr. 2020.
Domizlaff, H. (2005). *Die Gewinnung des öffentlichen Vertrauens. Hamburg: Marketing Journal.* Gesellschaft für angewandtes Marketing mbH. (Originalwerk veröffentlicht 1939).
Fridays for Future Deutschland. (2023). Unsere Forderungen an die Politik. Fridays for Future. https://fridaysforfuture.de/forderungen/allgemein/. Accessed 19 Dec. 2023.
Gerken, G. (1994). *Die fraktale Marke.* Econ Verlag.

Heidegger, M. (1967). *Sein und Zeit*. Max Niemeyer Verlag Tübingen (Originalwerk veröffentlicht 1927).

Isaacson, W. (2023). *Elon Musk*. Simon & Schuster.

Kormann, C. (13 December 2019). The pure spirit of Greta Thunberg is the perfect antidote to Donald Trump. https://www.newyorker.com/news/news-desk/the-pure-spirit-of-greta-thunberg-is-the-perfect-antidote-to-donald-trump. Accessed 28 Apr. 2020.

Levinson, B. (1988). *Rain Man*. MGM/UA Communications Company.

Limburg, J. (2019). Is My Autism a Superpower? https://www.theguardian.com/society/2019/nov/03/is-autism-a-superpower-greta-thunberg-and-others-think-it-can-be. Accessed 23 Dec. 2020.

Kessler, G. (25. April 2019). Thunberg und die Kernkraft. Die Greta-Frage. https://energiewinde.orsted.de/klimawandel-umwelt/greta-thunberg-lehnt-atomenergie-ab. Accessed 29 Apr. 2020.

Meffert, H., Burmann, C., & Koers, M. (Eds.). (2002). *Markenmanagement*. Gabler.

Nietzsche, F. (1980ff). *Sämtliche Werke*. In: von G. Colli & M. Montinari (Hrsg.) *Kritische Studienausgabe* in 15 Bänden, herausgegeben. DTV de Gruyter. Zitiert als „KSA". – KSA 4: Also sprach Zarathustra.

Panofsky, E. (2002). Et in Arcadia ego. In: von V. Breidecker (Hrsg.), *Poussin und die Tradition des Elegischen*. Friedenauer Presse.

Philips, T. (2019). *Joker*. Warner Bros. Pictures.

Rovell, D. (2 June 2018). Roger Federer leaves Nike for Uniqlo apparel. https://www.espn.com/tennis/story/_/id/23972357/roger-federer-wears-uniqlo-apparel-wimbledon-opener-ending-apparel-deal-nike. Accessed 29 Apr. 2020.

Sartre, J.-P. (1991). *Das Sein und das Nichts, Reinbeck bei Hamburg:* Rowohld Verlag (Originalwerk veröffentlicht 1943).

The Guardian. (29. Januar 2020). Greta Thunberg files application to trademark her name. https://www.theguardian.com/environment/2020/jan/29/greta-thunberg-files-application-to-trademark-her-name. Accessed 29 Apr. 2020.

Thunberg, G. (2019). *No One Is Too Small to Make a Difference*. (Kindle Edition). Penguin.

Vagianos, A. (17 April 2019). Teen Climate Activist Greta Thunberg to EU Lawmakers: 'I Want You To Panic'. https://www.huffpost.com/entry/teen-climate-activist-greta-thunberg-to-eu-lawmakers-i-want-you-to-panic_n_5cb-7344ce4b0ffefe3ba6287. Accessed 20 Dec. 2020.

Waller, S. (2015). *Leben in Entlastung. Mensch und Naturzweck bei Arnold Gehlen*. UVK Verlag.

Woodward, A. (3 January 2020). Greta Thunberg Turns 17 Today. Here's How She Started a Global Climate Movement in Just 18 Months.https://www.businessinsider.sg/greta-thunberg-bio-climate-change-activist-2019-9?r=US&IR=T. Accessed 3 May 2020.

6

BP: On This Side of Good and Evil

Abstract Not only in Social Compliance Statements does it become apparent that companies and therefore their brands bear moral responsibility. This also comes to the fore whenever they come under public criticism. Given the severity with which criticism is often leveled, its relative consequencelessness for companies and brands can be quite surprising. The moving story of BP shows us in this regard that it is a characteristic of large brands to stand, in doubt, outside of moral responsibility.

The Biblical myth of expulsion from paradise is associated with the knowledge of good and evil and the accompanying moral responsibility of mankind. According to the Old Testament tradition, anyone who knows ethical categories is similar to God in this respect, but can no longer live like an animal in paradisiacal indifference to the world's injustices. Since divine insight into the right action is not given to us along with moral problem-awareness, ethical questions are among the most difficult. Despite the greatest efforts in this field, the persistent problem is that there is no foundation of morality that convinces all people equally.

In response to all attempts at moral justification, it is therefore *Friedrich Nietzsche's* endeavor to expose universally binding moral concepts as mere expressions of historical-social developments (cf. Nietzsche KSA 5, p. 245 ff.). Even this often harsh critic of all ethical and also epistemological objectivity agrees with most other thinkers in the assumption that, if one assumes a monotheistic God, this God himself cannot commit moral transgressions. There is a long discussion, particularly fueled by the Lisbon earthquake in

1755 and conducted under the term *theodicy problem*, about whether the disaster in the world can be reconciled with the assumption of omniscience, omnipotence, and infinite goodness of the Christian God. This problem can only be convincingly solved by denying all moral restrictions on divine action: Either one gives up faith entirely, or as a believer one adopts an agnostic attitude towards an absolute responsibility of God that is beyond good and evil measured by our standards. In both cases, the monotheistic God cannot be held morally accountable.

The same applies to the polytheistic pantheon of antiquity. No matter how similar these gods may seem to us, their often ethically questionable behavior eludes our moral judgment because we are merely mortal beings. Apart from this essential difference, which applies equally tomonotheism, the question of the moral responsibility of the ancient gods does not arise because they are revered as both the cause and protector of adversity in the world. For example, *Poseidon* is not only the god of the sea but also the god of earthquakes and, moreover, responsible for stability on the mainland. For him, as for all other ancient gods, the statement of the poet *Statius,*shared by the enlightened philosophers of antiquity, applies that fear first brought these gods into the world: "Primus in orbe deos fecit timor"—"Fear was the first to create gods here on earth." (Kudla, 2007, p. 111). People therefore created the gods out of fear of the threats in the world, which they then attributed to the respective deities themselves. However, the ancient gods were not there to hold them accountable for the disasters they caused. Instead, they serve to appease them so that no further harm befalls one. On the one hand, the gods *relieve* one of one's own guilt, which could consist, for example, in not having protected oneself enough—and on the other hand, the intimate relationship with the gods conveys the relieving feeling of being spared from future disasters. As symbolic perpetrators and also symbols of insurance against the disasters they are responsible for, they thus stand beyond moral judgment of good and evil.

The name of the oil platform "Deepwater Horizon" stands for one of the largest man-made environmental disasters to date, which began with its explosion on April 20, 2010, and the subsequent sinking of the drilling rig two days later (cf. Deepwater Horizon, 2023; Deepwater Horizon Explosion, 2023). As a result of this severe accident, which immediately claimed 11 lives, an estimated 4.9 million barrels of crude oil flowed from the open drilling rig into the sea over 87 days (cf. Deepwater Horizon Oilspill, 2023). The resulting environmental damage and economic losses around the Gulf of Mexico are still not foreseeable more than 10 years after the accident. The ongoing and to date over $54 billion expenditures for cleaning, compensation, and penalty payments confirm the sad record of this disaster (ibid.).

The image loss for the energy giant *British Petrol* (BP), as the operator of *Deepwater Horizon*, responsible for these immense damages, is estimated in the same dimensions. Particularly piquant is that the BP brand had undergone a much-noticed transformation process towards an environmentally conscious, green energy corporation in the previous decade. Up to this turning point in corporate strategy, communicated with a comprehensive redesign of the brand in 2000, BP can look back on a long history as a traditional energy corporation. This history dates back to the founding of the *Anglo Persian Oil Company* for the exploitation of oil deposits in today's Iraq in 1909 (cf. BP, 2023). Even though the APOC was not renamed British Petroleum Company until 45 years later, in 1954, it marketed its products under the brand name *British Petrol* in the United Kingdom from 1917 onwards (cf. BP Early History 2023). The logo *"BP"*, designed in the 1920s and distinguished by its characteristic serifs, shapes the face of the brand throughout the 20th century. In 1930, the letters, which had been in quotation marks until then, were freed from these and instead surrounded by a shield. Its green base with yellow initials and outline, established from 1947, still dictate BP's corporate colors today. While the first BP logo was designed by A.R. Saunders, an employee of BP unknown as a designer, the famous product and brand designer *Raymond Loewy* took care of the second redesign of the logo in 1961, which was modernized in form and color once again by *Siegel & Gale* in 1989. The logo now appears in a radiant green and the signet and border in solid yellow. This creates a generally fresher impression, reminiscent of a bed of daffodils due to its strong contrasts. Despite all changes, the BP logo remains constant in its different incarnations in the 20th century, standing with a defensive shield and stable initials for the unshakeable self-confidence of a major brand in the key industry of progress driven by oil.

In comparison, the company logo designed by the agency *Landor* in 2000 is to be understood as a visual break with tradition. The impression of a complete new start is created mainly by the fact that the initials, which had characterized the company's coat of arms for over three-quarters of a century, are banished. No longer standing in the optical center of events, they now only function as a comment, shrunk to lowercase, on the structural change of the company. In this new form, the lowercase letters *bp* are not only to stand for the proud tradition of British Petrol, but also for the new direction of the company encapsulated in the slogan *beyond petroleum* (Landor, 2015). Following the words of BP's then CEO, *Lord John Browne,* this path is a guilt-conscious departure from the company's unquestioned participation in climate change: "Ladies and gentlemen, climate change is a reality and we are partly responsible." (Cross, 2000). This will to shift the focus of one's own company from fossil to renewable energy in the face of the pressing climate problem already at the turn of the millennium is also reflected in the new logo for *beyond petroleum*, bearing the name of the Greek sun god *Helios* (BP, 2020). This logo, reminiscent at first glance of the Pril flowers popular with the children of the 70s, combines the floral references of the corporate colors laid out in the last version of the BP logo with a symbol standing for the power of the sun. The interplay of the existing color scheme with a newly added shade of green symbolizes the transition from sunrays to renewable green raw materials.

This rather bold reinterpretation of the brand's appearance is supported by a campaign conceived by *Ogilvy*, which openly names the structural change. The posters, designed in sober white, are conceived as "messages, not ads" (Bowen, 2005) according to the statements of the art director *K.J. Bowen*, and live from the surprise effect that an oil producer addresses the pressing question of alternative energy sources. In addition, highlights on the posters, especially with statements like "It's time to think *outside* the barrel" and "It's time for fuel to *come clean*" (ibid.), deliberately address an internal cleansing process in the company. In this way, with this campaign, BP also professes internal conversion and purification, which have led to a change of thinking.

The accompanying intention to rethink energy is also supported by information on energy consumption on BP's website. In addition, the print campaign and the individual *Carbon-Footprint-Calculator* provided online by BP at the time contribute to popularizing the term *carbon footprint* and thus also strengthening general awareness of climate change. The TV campaign builds on the accompanying shift in consciousness by showing people in interview situations who react surprised, amazed, and curious to questions about climate change and renewable energies. Indeed, the message that an energy giant has recognized the signs and is ready to do the right thing resonates. The rebranding campaign and the green image appeal to a broad public, which also seems to have an extremely positive effect on brand image and business figures:

> "Sales from 2004 to 2005 rose from $192 billion to $240 billion then to $266 billion in 2006. Moreover, a Landor Associates survey of consumers found that 21% of them thought BP was the greenest of oil companies, followed by Shell at 15% and Chevron at 13%. The campaign also won a 2007 gold Effie

from the American Marketing Association. BP said that from 2000-2007, its brand awareness went from 4 percent to 67 percent." (Nastu, 2008)

This enormous prestige gain of the brand through the new green image reaches its peak in April 2010, when BP is ranked 34th among the world's most valuable brands by the rating agency *BrandZ*, ahead of all other energy corporations (Ranking the Brands BP, 2023). However, this positive assessment changes abruptly with the disaster in the Gulf of Mexico. In 2010, BP recorded a loss in the valuation of the brand value estimated at around 1 billion US dollars (Rao, 2010) and fell out of the TOP 100 global brands of the rating agency Interbrand for the first time in 11 years in the fall of the same year (Sweeney, 2010).

The accompanying loss of reputation of the corporation and brand finds its visual expression in a redesign competition for the BP logo announced by *Greenpeace* as early as the end of June 2010, the submissions of which accuse the corporation of significant greenwashing and greed for money. The most commonly used stylistic element is the contrasting of the yellow-green company logo with black and brown oil stains. The use of the biohazard symbol in or instead of the Helios logo is also quite popular. At the same time, there are many creative ideas on how the term of the insincere environmental sinner can be reduced to the abbreviation "bp": "Beyond promises", "blooming propaganda" or even more crudely "bunch of pricks" are just a few of these diverse possibilities (The Guardian, 2010). The message cast in word and image into the language of advertising could not be clearer: The environmental disaster reveals the true face of a classic energy corporation, whose turn to new energies is nothing more than a PR trick. A comment on the PR-Watch website puts this accusation in a nutshell:

> "To BP I say, you have fooled the American Consumer with your bullshit adds about being a green company. It is very evident based on the fact that you no longer refer to 'Beyond Petroleum' on your web page, that you are now finally aware that both myself and many other American who have kept their eyes open over the last ten years are now fully aware that you are NOT Beyond Petroleum, instead you are British Petroleum: A London based multinational OIL/Petroleum company that is much more interested in short term profits than in 'saving the planet' with your uneconomical solar voltaic cells and wind power." (Cottages, 2010).

Indeed, the slogan *beyond petroleum* disappears from the website and all other advertising materials of the corporation immediately after the disaster.

Not directly related to this and largely following the general development in the energy sector, BP also withdraws on a large scale from its commitment to wind power and solar energy during this phase and focuses much more on fossil energies in the coming years (David, 2013). Despite this return to the old core business, however, the corporation still holds on to presenting itself as a brand interested in green energies, and to a greater extent than in 2010. According to BrandZ, by 2019 the financial burdens of the disaster in the Gulf of Mexico for BP have been overcome and the environmental damage has been forgotten to such an extent that the corporation can convince with its campaign again focusing on alternative energies:

> "Nearing the end of the financial impact from the Deepwater Horizon environmental disaster in the Gulf of Mexico, almost a decade ago, BP is invested in growth and brand communication. With the campaign 'We see possibilities everywhere', BP asserts that it can help the world keep advancing many ways, including with natural gas and solar." (Schept, 2019).

The BP 2019 Annual Report also highlights the outlook for the company's net CO_2 emissions to be reduced to zero by 2050: "Our ambition is to be a net zero company by 2050 or sooner and to help the world get to net zero." (BP p.l.c., 2020). However, the same objections seem to be valid against this rhetoric, which were already made before the disaster in the Gulf of Mexico regarding BP's small investments of only 4% in sustainable energies (cf. Democracy Now, 2010). In fact, in 2019, the company made its profits exclusively from gas and oil and losses from the alternative energy sources included in the balance sheet item "all other business areas" (BP p.l.c., 2020). In relation to this, the combined revenues from oil and gas exceeded the other business areas by about 150 times (ibid.) in 2019. The new slogan used here, *keep advancing*, is not dissimilar to the once motto *beyond petrol* and can be understood as a renewed confirmation of the accusation of greenwashing and the arbitrariness of the commitment to sustainability raised before 2010. This accusation is also evident in details, such as the bars for gas and oil in a graph on the future development of energy sources, which are kept in BP green in the 2020 annual report. This color scheme almost suggests it as a sign of sustainability and environmental friendliness that the demand for fossil energies will continue to grow in the future, according to BP's estimate. The coal not exploited by BP itself, on the other hand, is presented in a brown-grayish color tone, following the same logic as most Greenpeace-BP logos, and thus branded as a much *dirtier* energy source. In view of this, Robert Brulle, Professor of Environmental

Sociology at Drexel University, emphasized in 2019: "The bigger picture is that BP is still investing 97 percent of its business in oil. The rest is lipstick on a pig" (Farand, 2019).

In view of this obvious imbalance, this campaign focusing on new energies should be no more successful than the BP brand has steadily lost prestige since 2010. At first glance, the aforementioned slump in the valuation of the brand value seems to support this thesis. However, BP had previously staged a rally in brand value, with the brand rising from 93rd place among the world's most valuable brands in 2007 to 34th place in spring 2010 at BrandZ. After the disaster, however, it is still in 64th place in this ranking in 2011, clearly above the 2007 placement (Ranking the Brands, 2023). From 2016, BP disappears from the BrandZ Top 100 ranking. A comparable decline is also evident in the general development of other top brands since 2010. This is mainly due to the fact that companies from the digital sector are increasingly conquering the top positions, while companies from traditional sectors such as the energy sector can no longer maintain their positions. This development is also evident in the placement of the competitor *Shell*, which slips from 40th to 65th place at BrandZ between 2010 and 2019 (Ranking the Brands Shell, 2023). In contrast to these declining ratings in relative comparison to other sectors, the rating agency Brand Finance records a steady and parallel gain in brand value in its 2020 annual report, both for BP and Shell between 2013 and 2019 (Brand Finance, 2020). In 2023, BP ranks 7th among the world's most valuable energy brands according to BrandFinance (Brand Finance, 2023).

In summary, these assessments of brand value suggest that the development of BP's brand ranking after the disaster has much to do with general shifts in the world's top brands and developments in the oil industry. In addition, an overvaluation of the brand by analysts due to the euphoria of the *beyond petrol campaign* until spring 2010 seems likely, which has fallen back to a more realistic value in the aftermath of the Deepwater Horizon disaster. Following this assessment, one can argue that the brand has suffered little from the disaster and its consequences, despite all contrary assessments.

The reason for this in the clever communication of the corporation and a forgetful or indifferent public towards environmental damage does not really have to convince. Rather, one can say that the public is quite environmentally conscious and media competent enough to recognize such diversionary tactics. It is more likely that the green veneer is welcomed by many consumers in silent agreement. This consideration makes sense if one assumes that consumers, despite increasing environmental awareness, still largely assume that they will be dependent on fossil fuels and thus on the consumption of the products of traditional energy companies for an indefinite period. Mindful of the environmental damage and the associated moral dubiousness of one's own lifestyle, a brand like BP provides a *relief* for the individual conscience in the sense that it glosses over the environmental damage both during production and consumption of its own products through communication, product design, and appealing distribution channels.

More important than the beautiful appearance of the brand associated with the accusation of greenwashing seems to be the symbolic protective function of the brand against consumer responsibility. Just as one once needed a god responsible for the preservation and damage of earthquakes and stability, large brands seem to be useful in the face of one's own oil dependency, by taking on the symbolic responsibility for the smooth preservation as well as the guilt for the effects of one's own lifestyle on the environment. In this worldly interaction with the oil giant, one could therefore speak of a silent agreement between the brand and its customers. The first part of this unspoken agreement is that the brand takes full moral responsibility for an environmental disaster like the one in the Gulf of Mexico. One's own lifestyle based on fossil fuels does not have to be questioned because we can point to brands like BP as a symbol of the exploitation of nature and thus the cause of impending climate change. Given the existing demand for climate-damaging crude oil products, the second unspoken agreement is that this moral responsibility is as inconsequential in the public's imagination as that of a Greek god. Just as *Poseidon* is held responsible for both stability and earthquakes, it is accepted that the brand responsible for one's own energy supply also causes environmental pollution. However, the knowledge of this leads no more today than it did thousands of years ago to turn away from those responsible. Rather, it requires this entity, which serves as a symbol for both the smooth running of existing conditions and their destructive side effects. Loud criticism of BP, for example, also supports this agreement insofar as it emphasizes the role assigned to the energy giant, as well as confirming the *relief* of the individual conscience. A not to be underestimated burden, on the other hand, would be having to share the responsibility attributed to the brand for the environmental damage caused by one's own consumption. From this perspective, delegating responsibility to a worldly brand that operates beyond good and evil can be understood as a necessary cultural technique which *relieves* the individual from the demands of constant reflection on their consumer behavior and, by extension, their existence in modern society.

In view of this, BP's renewed strategy of a communication strategy focusing on environmentally friendly and renewable energies does not necessarily seem comprehensible. One could take the position that the branding of the energy giant is secondary due to the ongoing demand for fossil fuels and a brand appearance perceived as insincere greenwashing also causes more harm than good. However, one can also realize that the silent agreement can only exist if there is a demand for the product. Even if the complete abandonment of oil should still be some distance away, with this development, the traditional oil companies identified exclusively with fossil energies will no longer be able to exist in their symbolic function as a brand. In view of this, it is essential for the future strength of the BP brand, despite all foreseeable and justified criticism, to continue to pursue a strategy that, although with a new slogan, is just as much aimed at the time after the end of the current business model as the rebranding as *beyond petroleum* was.

References

Bowen, K. J. (2005). Clients: BP. http://kjbowen.com/clients/bp/. Accessed 19 Dec. 2023.

BP. (16 December 2023). https://en.wikipedia.org/wiki/BP. Accessed 19 Dec. 2023.

BP. (24 July 2020). Helios at 20. https://www.bp.com/en/global/corporate/news-and-insights/reimagining-energy/helios-at-20.html. Accessed 20 Dec. 2023.

BP p.l.c. (2020). Energy with purpose. BP Annual Report and Form 20-F 2019 [PDF]. https://www.bp.com/content/dam/bp/business-sites/en/global/corporate/pdfs/investors/bp-annual-report-and-form-20f-2019.pdf. Accessed 17 June 2023.

Brand Finance. (2020). Oil and gas 50 2019 ranking. https://brandirectory.com/rankings/oil-and-gas/2019. Accessed 19 Dec. 2023.

Brand Finance. (2023). Branddirectory OIL and GAS 50. 2023 ranking. https://brandirectory.com/rankings/oil-and-gas/table. Accessed 19 Dec. 2023.

Cottages, A. (3 July 2010). Beyond petroleum what a farce. https://www.prwatch.org/comment/9690#comment-9690. Accessed 20 Jan. 2024.

Cross, M. (25 July 2000). BP rebrands on a global scale. *The Guardian*. https://www.theguardian.com/business/2000/jul/25/bp. Accessed 20 Jan. 2023.

David, J. E. (22 April 2013). ‚Beyond Petroleum' No more? BP goes back to basics. https://www.cnbc.com/id/100647034. Accessed 20 Dec. 2023.

Deepwater Horizon. (19 November 2023). https://en.wikipedia.org/wiki/Deepwater_Horizon. Accessed 19 Dec. 2023.

Deepwater Horizon Explosion. (15 December 2023). https://en.wikipedia.org/wiki/Deepwater_Horizon_explosion. Accessed 19 Dec. 2023.

Deepwater Horizon Oilspill. (2 December 2023). https://en.wikipedia.org/wiki/Deepwater_Horizon_oil_spill. Accessed 19 Dec. 2023.

Democracy Now. (5. May 2010). BP funnels millions into lobbying to influence regulation and rebrand image, an Interview with Antonia Juhasz. https://www.democracynow.org/2010/5/5/bp_funnels_millions_into_lobbying_to. Accessed 11 June 2023.

Farand, C. (29 January 2019). BP's first global advertising campaign since deepwater horizon accused of being ‚deceptive and hypocritical'https://www.desmogblog.com/2019/01/29/bp-first-global-advertising-campaign-deepwater-horizon-accused-greenwashing-deceptive. Accessed 19 Dec. 2023.

Kudla, H. (2007). *Lexikon der lateinischen Zitate*. C.H. Beck.

Landor. (2015). Brand as a Beacon of Change. https://web.archive.org/web/20150929035511/https://landor.com/work/bp. Accessed 20 Dec. 2023.

Nastu, J. (15 January 2008). 'Beyond Petroleum' Pays Off For BP. https://www.environmentenergyleader.com/2008/01/beyond-petroleum-pays-off-for-bp/. Accessed 10 Jan. 2023.

Nietzsche, F. (1980ff). Sämtliche Werke. In: von G. Colli & M. Montinari (Eds.), *Kritische Studienausgabe in 15 B.d., herausgegeben DTV de Gruyter*. Zitiert als „KSA". – KSA 5: Jenseits von Gut und Böse. Zur Genealogie der Moral.

Ranking the Brands. (2023). BP. https://www.rankingthebrands.com/Brand-detail.aspx?brandID=132. Accessed 19 Dec. 2023.

Rao, L. (22 June 2010). Report: BP's brand value plunges by nearly $1 Billion. TechCrunch. https://techcrunch.com/2010/06/21/bp-brand-value/. Accessed 20 Jan. 2024.

Schept, K. (2019). BrandZ: Top 100 Most Valuable Global Brands 2019. https://www.anda.cl/wp-content/uploads/2020/04/BZ_Global_2019_WPP_compressedv2.pdf. Accessed 19 Dec. 2023.

Solnit, R. (23 August 2021). Big Oil Coined 'Carbon Footprints' to Blame Us for Their Greed. Keep Them on the Hook. https://www.theguardian.com/commentisfree/2021/aug/23/big-oil-coined-carbon-footprints-to-blame-us-for-their-greed-keep-them-on-the-hook. Accessed 20 Dec. 2023.

Statista. (2020). Dossier zum Thema BP p.l.c. https://de.statista.com/statistik/studie/id/20914/dokument/bp-plc-statista-dossier/. Accessed 20 Dec. 2023.

Sweney, M. (16 September 2010). BP Falls Out of Index of Top 100 Brands After Deepwater Horizon Oil Spill.https://www.theguardian.com/media/2010/sep/16/apple-iphone-interbrand. Accessed 20 Dec. 2023.

The Guardian. (10 June 2010). In Pictures: Greenpeace Competition to Redesign the BP Logo.https://www.theguardian.com/environment/gallery/2010/jun/10/greenpeace-bp-logo-competition. Accessed 20 Dec. 2023.

7

Opel: Who We Are

Abstract Opel was long perceived as the car brand of skilled workers and lower-level employees. When their living environment and thus the sales of the Opel brand came under pressure, the car manufacturer embarked on an image change that was supposed to redefine the identity of the brand. However, it remains uncertain to this day how far the Opel myth can still inspire contemporary vehicles. This exemplifies that a positive image change is only possible based on a convincing handling of one's own identity.

One of the most controversial theorems in the philosophy of *Hegel* is the early mention in the dispute with *Schelling* and *Fichte* of the "identity of identity and non-identity" (Hegel Works, Vol. 2, p. 96). This formulation indeed seems to break with the law of contradiction, which states that a statement cannot be accepted simultaneously with its negation. However, Hegel is by no means trying to override the laws of two-valued logic. Rather, he is pointing out that the formal-logical determination of identity in the manner of "A is identical with itself", briefly "A = A", can say nothing about the identity in the sense of the *being* of something (cf. Hegel Works, Vol. 6, p. 41 ff.). Satisfactory answers to the question of being can only be found in the identification of a thing with other facts that are not identical with it in this sense. This happens, for example, when we answer the question "What is a rose?" not with the formally true statement, "A rose is a rose", but with the following definition: "A rose is a specimen of the plant genus that gives its name to the family of rose plants". Following Hegel's argument, identity is thus determined by non-identity in the manner of "A is B, C, D …".

From this, it is also understandable that we can only describe our own *self* with non-identical terms. I am not simply *I*, but for example intelligent, diligent, brave, a member of the shooting club, and much more. We also learn about ourselves in terms of these and other descriptions only in interaction with other people and thus actually from the perspective of non-identical selves. *George Herbert Mead* describes this connection well over a hundred years after Hegel with his concept of *self-consciousness* as an integral of "I" and "me":

> "The "I" is the response of the organism to the attitudes of the others; the "me" is the organized set of attitudes of others which one himself assumes." (Mead, 1934, p. 175).

This model, in turn, is based on the assumption of the identity of identity and non-identity, in that self-consciousness and personality are based on the fact that we refer to ourselves both from the immediate perspective as subject, "I", and from the assumed perspective as object for others, "me".

Analogous to this determination of self-consciousness, the problem of integrating external and internal perspectives also arises for the question of the identity of brands, as a look at *identity-based brand management* illustrates (cf. Burmann et al., 2012). This approach sees itself as a synthesis of previous theories of brand management, which understand brands either one-sidedly from the brand image or from the brand identity. Understanding the brand from the image perspective aims to improve the brand based on knowledge of the public perspective on the brand. Brand management thus essentially consists in recognizing the image of the brand in the *external* public perception and activating knowledge about it in the internal processes for controlling the brand image. In contrast, there are those approaches that start with brand identity, under which they subsume all elements of a brand that emerge from the institution of the brand owner. This includes product and brand design as well as all organizational and ideal aspects that determine the perception of the brand from the perspective of the *internal community*. The task of brand management is then to start with the individual elements of brand identity and control the brand image from there. Following the insight that starting with the *brand identity* is promising but tends to be as one-sided as the approach from the *brand image*, identity-based brand management has emerged as a position that, starting from the internal perspective of brand identity, also includes the elements constituting the brand from the external perspective on the brand image.

Seemingly as in Mead's reconstruction of self-consciousness, the actual identity of the brand here is understood as emerging from the interplay of identity, the "I" of the inner perspective, and the non-identical "Me" of the outer perspective. Upon closer inspection, however, this approach can only provide limited insight into the understanding of brand identity. While this division is correct and useful for highlighting the different perspectives of those directly involved in the brand's organization and the public, it is the point of Mead's "I" that it is directly connected with the self-reflecting consciousness. Therefore, it would be wrong to describe "brand identity" as the "internal reflection of one's own actions" of those institutionally involved in the brand (Burmann et al., 2012, p. 28). Indeed, the community within the organization deals with the brand with greater interest, commitment, and scope for action than the public. However, none of the participants could claim to be this one, self-reflecting consciousness of the brand *itself*. Rather, each of the actors involved here also takes a subjective perspective on the image of the brand's identity, which lies outside their own consciousness and is to be understood as a "self" in a transferred sense. Since this does not coincide with their self-consciousness, brand identity must be understood as a third instance, distinct from both the perspective of consumers and the internal community. It can be realized that the strength of big brands lies precisely in the fact that such an independent brand identity, standing between the participants, has been permanently established, to which all those inside and outside the organization can relate as a self mediated by certain external insignia. *Hans Domizlaff* refers to this as the "independence of the life of brands, which can continue to grow completely independently of the critical mind of individual individuals" (Domizlaff, 1939/2005, p. 150).

A useful model for the genesis and significance of such a conception of brand identity is provided by Arnold Gehlen's *concept of institutions*. He describes institutions as behaviors that have developed over longer periods and have become habitual, whose identity is conveyed to people both internally and externally in contact with it through certain images. For him, it is of utmost importance that this identification does not arise through purpose-rational processes. Rather, these images are the products of human imagination, which is not organized rationally, and they convey certain ideas by affecting us on an emotional level. An important aspect is that this feeling is to be understood as an elevation and *self-enhancement* of the individual human being. Since archaic times, identification with these signs of the "non-I" (Gehlen, 1950/1993, p. 496 f.) has given humans the feeling of growing beyond themselves (cf. Waller, 2015, p. 55 f.).

Noteworthy also for the analysis of brands is that Gehlen distinguishes between the motives for action evoked by identification with images on the one hand, and the rational purposes of an institution on the other. According to his theory, exemplified fundamentally by totemism, institutional action is indeed associated with certain actions aimed at rational purposes. At the same moment, however, we must understand these functional behaviors in their genesis as by-products of group-related habits, whose by no means purpose-rational processes are motivated by emotionally charged images. Following this analysis, totemism, for example led to animal breeding as a by-product: interested in completely different motives and oriented towards the image of the animal, its rituals go hand in hand with the enclosure of animals (cf. Gehlen, 1950/1993, p. 475). This relationship describes a balance in which emotion and purposefulness support each other. With this in mind, it can also be said that if social rational purposes are lost, the non-rational emotional motives that stabilize them also disappear. Those who no longer practice animal breeding, therefore, lose the emotional motives and images related to the traditional way of life.

Not only the fact that brand formation is also based significantly on the difference between symbolic and functional aspects of the product suggests a connection to the archaic behaviors described by Gehlen. For example, when we buy automobiles of the brands *Jaguar* or *Ferrari*, the selection of animalistic image motifs already reminds us of the possibility of separating motive and purpose as just described with regard to early humans. The mere functional movement from A to B is a by-product of the actual emotional fusion of the own ego with the machine and thus also the properties of the modern totem animal that takes place in the cockpit of the automobile. As automobiles are machines of physical empowerment of the individual *par excellence*, the emotional identification with the brand exceeds that of its functional value, not only in the case of luxury models. Rather, the preferences for certain car brands reflect the emotional self-enhancement and group affiliation of the individual, which are retrospectively reinforced by the purchase of the vehicle.

A perhaps not immediately obvious example of this is the brand *Opel*, which held a prominent position in the Federal Republic of Germany just a few decades ago. Indeed, probably no car brand in Germany has symbolized the group affiliation of a social class to the extent that was once the case with the Opel brand. The brand reflected both the pride in what had been achieved and the possibility of making something of oneself in post-war West Germany through one's own hard work. The black Opel lightning bolt on a yellow background was thus the *non-self*, in the face of which the self-confidence of the lower middle class grew beyond itself. Indeed, the often glossed-over class differences in the early ear of the Federal Republic can be identified by the groups that had a rather affirmative or pejorative relationship to them. *Helmut Kohl* would probably never have arrived in an Opel, and when the weekly newspaper DIE ZEIT reported in 2020 that *Rudi Assauer* at the end of his life was little more than an "old Opel", it also underlines the social class and life world from which the legendary Schalke 04 manager originated (cf. Willek, 2020).

It was in the midst of its heyday, when the Opel logo took on the basic shape of a lightning bolt, flattened at the ends and lying horizontally, cutting through a circle with the same line thickness, with the redesign in 1970 At this time, about 20% of the newly registered cars in Germany came from the car manufacturer, which had been owned by the American automotive giant *General Motors* since the Great Depression of the early 1930s (Opel, 2023). The fact that the brand, with minor fluctuations, covered this fifth of new registrations from the early 1950s to the early 1980s, demonstrates its outstanding importance in the German car market, which was developing with the economic miracle (ibid.). During this core phase, the brand could boast a product range that began with the compact cars *Kadett* and *Ascona* in the middle class and covered the entire demand spectrum via *Rekord* in the upper middle class, up to the KAD models *Kapitän, Admiral* and *Diplomat* in the upper class (cf. Hrachowy, 2017, p. 10 ff.). During this phase, the brand, which has been producing cars since 1899, has built an image that is in no way inferior to the slogan "the reliable one", later "tested reliability", first used in 1936. The standard models are unexciting and conservative, representing the German virtue of high quality standards. On the other hand, the DNA of the parent company GM is clearly evident in the models of the upper middle class and upper class, whose design reminiscent of American cruisers has a quite sophisticated appearance. Still, these prestige models cannot compete with the saturated image and the technical performance of the brand *Mercedes-Benz*, which dominates the upper class in Germany, and are also not particularly strong sellers. Nevertheless, they round off the image of Opel as a broadly positioned, full-fledged car brand, whose myth stands for social security and the dream of social advancement (Hrachowy, 2017, p. 33).

Looking from this perspective at the reasons why Opel began a decline from the beginning of the 1980s, reaching only 10% by the turn of the millennium and just over 6% of new registrations in Germany in 2021 (Opel, 2023), these seem to be closely linked to the growing threats to this way of life during these years. This development can be described *in nuce* as follows: in response to the oil crisis of the early 70s and the success of the *VW Golf*, Opel withdrew from the upper class with the end of the KAD series and focused on the segments below, the small car and compact class. With this strategy, Opel was able to successfully assert itself against German and Japanese competition in the 1980s, and by the end of the decade was even the German car manufacturer with the highest return on sales (Hrachowy, 2017, p. 72). Higher returns, which in the long term had to come at the expense of quality, were also promised by the price stipulation policy for suppliers of the manager *José Ignacio López de Arriortúa*, who had been acting as purchasing manager since 1987. His cost-cutting course, as well as the renaming of the Kadett to Astra, which marked the end of the model names oriented towards naval ranks, and the final withdrawal from the upper middle class with the discontinuation of the Omega, led to Opel's reality becoming a negative reflection of its former brand image during the 90s. The vehicles showed some serious defects in workmanship, and the social elevator, previously embodied in the model names and the spread into all price segments, got stuck in the lower middle class.

In parallel, the situation of the company's own workforce shows that the social model of the old Federal Republic has become even more dramatically unstable. Quality problems and declining sales, financial obligations towards and disputes with the parent company GM, as well as production relocations abroad lead to job cuts and plant closures. In particular, the closure of the central Opel plant in Bochum in 2014 is a writing on the wall. This city, in the geographical and emotional center of the post-war industrial worker's world, the Ruhr area, no longer stands for the self-confidence of German industrial workers in general and Opel workers in particular, but for the impositions of industrial structural change in times of globalization (cf. Frenzel, 2012).

The fact that Opel has been in the headlines for years before this closure with reports of cuts, job losses, and labor disputes suggests the drastically falling sales figures in relation to other brands. Outside of the workforce threatened by unemployment at the former main plant, no one may want to join in the battle cry "We are Opel!" Indeed, the brand now has a pronounced "loser image," as *Stefan Bratzel*, director of the Center of Automotive

Management (CAM) at the University of Applied Sciences for Business in Bergisch-Gladbach emphasizes (Firlus, 2018). However, contrary to the statements made there, this was not "always" the case, but is a side effect of the upheavals in the world of work described above in recent decades. Also because the situation of Opel and its employees reflects the precarious situation that many workers and employees feel threatened by, it seems difficult for this clientele to still identify positively with the brand. By reflecting the risky situation of ordinary people, the once so proud brand has become almost infectious for a layer of society that no one wants to belong to.

In contrast, traditional brands like *Volkswagen* and *Audi* can establish themselves as brands for those who can keep up with the changing conditions of the mainstream or have even made the leap to a higher class. On the other hand, reissues of classics are gaining importance, which align with the general trend towards individualism as a response to the social structures of late modernity that are getting into a spin. Opel joined this trend in 2013 with the small car "Adam" produced in Eisenach. The name of the model, reminiscent of the company founder of the same name but pronounced in English [ˈædəm], represents a new beginning under the conditions of individualized and internationalized late modernity. The special feature of the retro-designed car is that it is delivered in literally thousands of different, online customizable personalizations in equipment and design elements. "One car. A thousand possibilities," is the accompanying slogan.

As much as this popular model reminds of successful reissues of small cars like the *Mini* produced under the direction of BMW since 2001 and the *Fiat 500* from 2007 (cf. Piper, 2012), it differs decisively in one respect: it is not a reissue of a classic, but a reinvention that wants to undo its own history with a leap into an imagined past. The aim is to start all over again, literally from the first human being. The fact that it *en passant* omits that the leader of the company at the time of the first Opel car was not the sewing machine manufacturer Adam Opel, but his wife Sophie after his death, appears as a missed opportunity for the brand. With a "Sophia," a different perspective on the brand's own past could have been opened up, taking into account the new awareness of gender roles. However, the impression remains of a quite popular model, whose invented retro design, however, falls behind comparable models and probably only gets the chance to become a real cult car as a *classic in spe* with the stop of production in 2019.

The problems shown here in repositioning as breaking aways from one's own history are even more reflected in the brand campaign "Umparken im Kopf" ("Re-parking in the head") from 2014, which started shortly after the introduction of the Adam. This campaign ignores the newly made fresh start, takes completely different paths, and interprets the lack of interest in Opel as a misunderstanding on the part of potential buyers, which needs to be corrected. This campaign, conceived by the Opel marketing director in collaboration with the agency *Scholz & Friends*, therefore aims to encourage people to reconsider the common prejudices against the Opel brand and to be convinced solely by the design and technical quality of the cars (cf. Kröger, 2014). This campaign is based on the accurate definition of a brand as a *positive prejudice* (cf. Zschiesche & Errichiello, 2013, p. 38 ff.; idem, 2018, p. 22 ff.) - however, under the condition that this has turned negative in the case of Opel. In his role as brand ambassador, *Jürgen Klopp* sums up the approach of the campaign at an Opel dealer conference: "This prejudice, that you can't drive Opel anymore… it's important to point that out, that's yesterday's news." (Opel Germany, 2014). The large-scale advertising campaign begins with anonymous posters, internet banners, and YouTube films that tease common misconceptions of everyday life, such as "When a bull sees red, it becomes aggressive. But bulls are colorblind." By later identifying itself as the sender of the previous ads with the ads "Is Opel still the way you think?" an analogy is made between these misconceptions and the prejudices against the brand (cf. Scholz & Friends, 2020). In the spots broadcast in parallel and held as reports from the car cockpit, TV celebrities and stars drive an Opel and in their testimonials, they anecdotally address the bad image of the brand they have been familiar with so far as a staid, low-quality car, only to be positively surprised by the quality of the respective car.

As cleverly as this campaign is set up, the designation as "one of the most successful automotive campaigns of our time" (Scholz & Friends, 2020), as well as the awards won by the agency, including the advertising and communication industry's award for efficient brand communication, *Effi*, do not seem justified in every respect. This impression is reinforced by the fact that one would not really assume that most of the more or less prominent protagonists of the spots would switch to an Opel of their own accord. Rather, one gets the feeling that they actively deny their actual opinion of the brand without wanting to give it up. The Opel brand still seems to be associated with a general negative prejudice that they themselves do not want to be associated with. Under these circumstances, the supposed always existing rejection or even ignorance of the brand appears more played than the recognition expressed in the spots. None of the *thirtysomethings* mention, for example, that Opel was indeed represented in their own social milieu, which one could assume given Opel's high market share until the end of the 1980s.

One explanation for this may be that their own social rise still goes hand in hand with no longer identifying with this brand, which symbolizes the petty bourgeois milieu of their own childhood. The Opel-driving father, uncle, grandfather is a private matter that is shamefully concealed because it is detrimental to the successful image. Re-parking in the head, in this sense, at best leads to repressing everything that the Opel brand has meant to one so far.

In addition to the expected return of the repressed, it is highly questionable to assume that consumers owe it to anyone or are even willing to actively work on adjusting their thoughts. This approach also overlooked the fact that the identity of a car brand cannot be built exclusively on technical details. As described above with reference to the institutional philosophy of Arnold Gehlen, the fascination of car brands arises from the happy coincidence of emotional motives and purposeful functionality. In this sense, it is not *only* about technology that inspires, but also about why it emotionally touches us.

If one were to summarize this campaign and the introduction of the Opel Adam, which was discontinued again in 2019, problematic new beginning would probably fit best, which initially also reflects the sale of the Opel brand to the French car manufacturer PSA in 2017 as a keyword. However, one could also say that this break with tradition is a blessing in the sense that the brand has freed itself from the negative aspects of its own history. As part of a successful European car manufacturer, it was also possible to leave behind the precarious image of the recent past to some extent. Although these circumstances also changed again soon, and after PSA in turn changed its owner, Opel has been part of the *Stellantis Group* since 2021. However, one can also be cautiously optimistic in view of this, as the car manufacturer in Germany has again achieved significant market share gains of almost 1.2 percentage points to about 6.2%, with the *Opel Corsa* being the best-selling small car in Germany in 2021 and 2022 (cf. Opel, 2021).

The striking external feature of Opel's recent developments is a relaunch of the corporate design in 2023, which is characterized by the introduction of a new house font and a new bright Opel yellow through a new interpretation of the logo. The previous, continuous lightning symbol in the center of a circle was replaced by two pointed, separate trapezoids that form the new signet when stacked on top of each other. The more dynamic brand appearance is intended to symbolize the step towards the electrification of Opel's entire vehicle fleet by 2028. Whether this redesign is necessary is open to debate (cf. Foley, 2023). Unmistakably, the two now separate ends of the lightning bolt again point to a deliberate brea from the past and a renewed determination to start anew. The strength of the brand will depend on how deep this graphically anticipated farewell cuts with the past. It is likely that a real new start can only succeed in not completely turning away, but only by referring back to non-identical predicates of the Opel brand and its history, by positively answering what Opel once was for its buyers and how the brand can continue to be this in the future - but differently.

References

Burmann, C. & Halaszovich, T. & Hemmann, F. (2012). *Identitätsbasierte Markenführung. Grundlagen – Strategie – Umsetzung – Controlling.* Springer Fachmedien.

Domizlaff, H. (2005). *Die Gewinnung des öffentlichen Vertrauens.* Hamburg: Marketing Journal. Gesellschaft für angewandtes Marketing mbH. (Originalwerk veröffentlicht 1939).

Firlus, Thorsten. (2018). Warum das Ende des Adam ein Problem werden könnte. https://www.wiwo.de/unternehmen/industrie/opel-stoppt-produktion-warum-das-ende-des-adam-ein-problem-werden-koennte/22997886.html. Accessed 20 Dec. 2023.

Foley, J. (28 June 2023). The New Opel Logo Feels Kind of... Unnecessary? Creative Bloq.. https://www.creativebloq.com/news/opel-logo%60%60. Accessed 20. Dec. 2023

Frenzel, V. (14 December 2012). Opel-Werk. Auslaufmodell Bochum. Der Tagesspiegel. https://www.tagesspiegel.de/wirtschaft/opel-werk-auslaufmodell-bochum/7518448-all.html. Accessed 20 Dec. 2023.

Gehlen, A. (1993). *Der Mensch. Seine Natur und seine Stellung in der Welt. In ders. Gesamtausgabe,* Bd. 3.1, herausgegeben von K.-S. Rehberg. Frankfurt am Main: Vittorio Klostermann. (Originalwerk veröffentlicht 1950).

Hegel, G. W. F. (1986). *Werke in 20 Bänden* (1st edn.). Suhrkamp Verlag. – Hegel Werke, Bd. 2: Jenaer Schriften 1801–1807. – Hegel Werke, Bd. 6: Wissenschaft der Logik II. Erster Teil. Die objektive Logik. Zweites Buch. Zweiter Teil. Die subjektive Logik.

Hrachowy, F. O. (2017). *Opel. Chronik eines Kampfes. Die Geschichte der Automarke seit 1970.* Verlag Edition Technikgeschichte.

Kröger, M. (27 February 2014). Opels Schrei nach Anerkennung. https://www.spiegel.de/wirtschaft/unternehmen/umparkenimkopf-de-opel-offenbar-urheber-der-kampagne-a-955843.html. Accessed 20 Dec. 2023.

Mead, G. H. (1934). Mind, Self, and Society. University of Chicago Press.

Opel. (18 December 2023). https://de.wikipedia.org/wiki/Opel. Accessed 20 Dec. 2023.

Opel. (5 January 2022). Opel gewinnt 2021 deutlich Marktanteile in Deutschland. https://www.media.stellantis.com/de-de/opel/press/opel-gewinnt-2021-deutlich-marktanteile-in-deutschland?adobe_mc_ref=. Accessed 20 Dec. 2023.

Opel Deutschland. (13 March 2014). Umparken im Kopf mit Jürgen Klopp. YouTube. https://www.youtube.com/watch?v=2Ap2g8___KU&t=4s. Accessed 20 Dec. 2023.

Piper, G. (7 November 2012). Der Opel Adam spielt mit den Farben. Hannoversche Allgemeine Zeitung. https://www.haz.de/Mehr/Auto-Verkehr/Uebersicht/Der-Opel-Adam-spielt-mit-den-Farben. Accessed 23 Dec. 2023.

Scholz & Friends. (2020). UMPARKEN IM KOPF: Das Comeback von Opel: Eine der erfolgreichsten Automobilkampagnen unserer Zeit. https://web.archive.org/web/20210730163526/http://s-f.com:80/arbeiten/case/opel-umparken-im-kopf/. Accessed 20 Dec. 2023.

Willek, S. (12 August 2020). Rudi Assauer. Wo ist sein Geld geblieben? Die Zeit. https://www.zeit.de/2020/34/rudi-assauer-demenz-vermoegen-fc-schalke-04. Accessed 15 Aug. 2023.

Zschiesche, A., & Errichiello, O. (2013). *Marke ohne Mythos*. GABAL Verlag.

Zschiesche, A., & Errichiello, O. (2018). *Marke statt Meinung*. GABAL Verlag.

8

Beyond Meat: What We Should Eat

Abstract Concerns about animal welfare, environmental pollution, and the climate impact of conventional agriculture make alternatives to meat consumption a significant issue of our time. The fact that large parts of society will probably not become vegetarian in the traditional sense does not mean that they are entirely opposed to meatless alternatives. Brands like Beyond Meat, which produce aesthetically and tastefully comparable products based on plants, target this. However, given their branding, the question arises as to how to position a meat alternative beyond the progressive milieu.

The film *L'aile ou la cuisse* by *Claude* Zidi (1976), which ran in German cinemas in the seventies under the title *Brust oder Keule (The Wing or the Thigh)*, is noteworthy not only because of the comedic performances of *Louis de Funès* and *Colouche* in their roles as father and son *Charles* and *Gérard Duchemin*. The grotesquely futuristic depiction of artificial food production in the factory of the villain *Jacques Trikatell* also creates a special appeal for the generation growing up in the late 1970s. Accompanied by de Funès' iconic "Oh!" and "Ah!", we witness how packaged fish and kitchen-ready chickens are created by spraying an artificial dough onto pre-made plastic skeletons and bones, pressing it into shape, and coloring it. Lettuce leaves are punched out of a continuous rubber band and bundled into heads. Chemical processes synthesize petroleum into red-colored pieces of meat.

By comparing the French cousin with the American-capitalist production method in the plot of the comedy, the industrially produced alternative to traditional meat consumption is portrayed as unnatural and unhealthy.

The focus is on motives that are also known as the "4 N arguments", statistically most often cited by meat eaters as reasons for its consumption: "Eating meat is natural, normal, necessary, and nice." (cf. Piazza et al., 2015). This unbroken positive attitude towards traditional eating habits may be due to the zeitgeist of the 1970s, when criticism of conventional food production was still a societal fringe phenomenon. It would probably have been difficult even for a comedian of Louis de Funès' stature to make fun of the synthetic production of food if he had not contrasted it with the gourmet restaurant, but with meat production as it takes place then and now all over the world in modern fattening farms. Anyone who knows the torment that fattening means for sentient beings, and who also understands that the climate catastrophe we are heading towards with open eyes is also caused by steadily increasing meat consumption, should have long lost their appetite for the wing or the thigh. For this person, it should be a moral duty to completely abstain from meat consumption.

Indeed, one of the biggest problems of moral philosophy can be demonstrated with this *ought*: the motivation for moral action does not necessarily correlate with the recognition of what is right and good. Generally speaking, humans are very good at recognizing grievances, but less good at following their own insight, especially when it comes to restrictions in their own lifestyle.

This very problem of motivation for good action is at the center of Kantian moral philosophy, which is also relevant in the context of the debate about meat consumption. *Immanuel Kant* assumes the possibility of an a priori knowledge of good action before any experience, just as he believes that this knowledge brings with it the motivation for the implementation of what has been recognized: "Duty is the necessity of an action out of respect for the law." (Kant, 1785, AA IV, p. 400). Anyone who recognizes their moral duty should be able to motivate them through an intellectually conditioned *feeling of respect* to align their actions with it (cf. Goy, 2007; Recki, 2006).

Without wanting to discuss a deontological justification for vegetarianism oriented towards Kant at this point, our eating habits are a suitable example that even the intellectual insight into the moral dimension of an action out of duty does not necessarily lead to ethically impeccable action. There are no statistics on the subject of Kantianism and vegetarianism. The author of these lines is at least an empirical proof that eating habits and intellectual insight into the categorical imperative do not have to correlate. He counts himself among those who, like the philosopher and public intellectual *Sam Harris*, cannot give a reasonable moral justification for the consumption of animals, but have nevertheless not become vegetarians (cf. Leenaert, 2014).

This finding is obviously embarrassing for an intelligent person due to its inconsistency; moreover, this attitude is *immoral* from a Kantian perspective. From his perspective, the world can be divided into such weak immoralists, who cannot make the decision for the morally right not due to lack of insight, but conscious capitulation to their inclinations. In contrast, there are moral people who are equipped with cognitive strength and a special sensitivity for moral duty, on the basis of which they muster the willpower to actually live vegan or at least vegetarian in this case.

Following their conscience, they may also feel obligated to persuade the faction of the ignorant and weak-willed to change their ways through educational work. Awareness campaigns, such as the one launched by the animal rights organization *Peta* in 2019 with the argument "Eating meat kills more animals than you think," drawing attention to the connection between meat consumption and the destruction of the rainforest, stand for this consistent stance (cf. Ried, 2019). In this campaign, the livestock themselves are spectacularly staged as predators, contrary to their actual dietary habits, tearing wild animals to feast on their flesh. As visually surprising and substantively convincing as the problem of the destruction of natural habitats by industrial meat production is presented, it is still likely that the campaign will lead to a change in thinking, but not necessarily to actual action. One is impressed and may rethink the connection between animal husbandry and environmental destruction, but this realization does not necessarily change one's own lifestyle.

Of course, the problem of lack of motivation through mere insight, which is evident here, has long been known in philosophical discourse. The founder of this perspective is *David Hume,* who historically, even before Kant, emphasized the primary role of emotion over reason in rejection of rationalist approaches: "Reason is, and ought only to be the slave of the passions, and can never pretend to any other office than to serve and obey them." (Hume, 1739–40/1978, T 2.3.3.4, SBN 415). With this often quoted insight, Hume assumes a fundamental motivation of people to follow their inclinations—and concludes that our intellectual apparatus is precisely adjusted to this. Thinking, therefore, serves to put our emotional motives into practice, not to generate the motivation for certain actions. This insight was later supplemented with a critical view of Kant, arguing that the thinking cannot do this through the recognition of imperatives of reason, which place themselves as duty between inclination and action.

On the contrary, the use of reason often goes hand in hand with justifying an already existing passion with rational arguments. The mentioned argumentation line of the 4 Ns of meat consumption seems to be structured in such a way that the desire for meat is the first and the respective argument is the subsequent second. In this sense, these superficially rational appearing arguments are close to mythical thinking, because they spin one's own preference into an emotionally colored narrative of naturalness, societal norms, concern for one's own health, and contribution to general satisfaction. One likes to eat meat and, not least out of shame for the associated acceptance of violence against animals, presents a narrative that justifies one's own actions. Against this background, it becomes clear that the aim of moving consumers to a diet that is beneficial to both animal welfare and the environment must not start with a change of thinking through arguments, but with an emotional reversal of thrust. People do not need to be taught better knowledge or even made to feel guilty—it is more about them really getting a *desire* to consume alternative products instead of meat.

When *Beyond Meat* made its IPO on the New York Stock Exchange in May 2019, it was not only the first IPO of a manufacturer of analogue meat on a purely plant-based basis; it was also one of the most successful stock market debuts since the year 2000 (cf. Market Watch, 2019). The company, founded by *Ethan Brown* in 2009, also joins the ranks of disruptive newcomers like *Uber* or *Tesla*, who are expected to completely reorganize an existing market at the beginning of the 21st century. Hence, the unexpectedly high price increase on the first trading day of Beyond Meat can then also be understood with the expectation of the company to shake up the established meat industry. This assumption is mainly based on the fact that, in contrast to classic vegetarian alternatives, everything about the product is designed to minimize the difference to real meat. With as little friction as possible, the consumer should not be aware that they are dealing with something other than real meat when consuming Beyond Meat.

Achieving this goal is not easy, even for a company solely dedicated to this problem. This is evident from the *Chicken Strips* by Beyond Meat, which were available in supermarkets from 2012 but only moderately successful outside the vegan community, and which disappeared from supermarket shelves by 2019 (see Andrews, 2019). More successful than this offer are the *Beyond Burgers* made from legumes, plant fats, potatoes, and beetroot, which provide an acceptable alternative to beef in both taste and texture (see Beyond Meat, 2023a). Currently, Beyond Meat sells meat analogues in various forms, whose red color is achieved by an impressive mimicry of beetroot blood, as well as new versions of chicken meat, including in the form of breaded pieces (see Beyond Meat, 2023b). In addition to the products marketed in supermarkets and directly to the end consumer via the website, Beyond Meat has also entered into partnerships with fast food chains that offer joint creations in their restaurants. One of the newer collaborations is *Beyond Fried Chicken,* which the fast food chain *Kentucky Fried Chicken* added to its menu in 2022 as a vegan alternative to fried chicken (see Lucas & Rogers, 2022).

However, Beyond Meat is not the only brand that has set itself the goal of perfectly imitating meat. In addition to other providers of meat alternatives, the company *Eat Just*, founded in 2011 under the name Hampton Creek, is taking a different approach to the new chicken nugget. Its products initially focus on alternatives to the use of eggs. The purely plant-based scrambled egg with the brand name *Just Egg*, which simulates taste and consistency based on mung beans, brings great success. The company's founder, Josh Tetrick, often repeats the story of his journey to becoming the successful CEO of a company that is valued at a possible volume of $3 billion even before a possible IPO (see Yu, 2021). His hero's story is about a young man with less than $3000 in his account, but with the firm will to found a company without his own scientific expertise that makes living animals unnecessary for the production of food (see CNBC International, 2021). Investors and employed food technologists help him to "find one from thousands of samples representing hundreds of plant species that magically stirs like an egg." (Just Egg, 2023). However, not only insiders of the company notice that this search may have been less extensive and the problem relatively easy to solve, as it is easily searchable in conventional vegan cookbooks. However, despite all criticism of the start-up founder's grandiose claims, it must be acknowledged that he has made vegan scrambled eggs attractive to those who are not already inclined towards a vegan diet—and who, according to the company's figures, have found a suitable analogue for them with a volume of already over 100 million replaced eggs:

> "We Make Our Eggs Right from the Earth—from Plants. With the #JUSTEgg Equivalent of 100 Million Eggs Sold, This Adds up to Real Savings for Our Environment. So We Want to Thank Our Planet, and to Thank You, for Getting Us to This Milestone toward Building a Better Food System." (@justegg, 2021).

The other product from Eat Just, which points even more clearly towards a revolution in meat consumption, is also based on a technique not entirely developed by the company itself. Under the brand name *Good Meat*, the company markets white meat pieces grown from stem cells and cultivated in a nutrient fluid, which share all essential properties with chicken meat, except for the need to slaughter an individual chicken for production.

In addition to this remarkable circumstance of sparing animals, the manufacturer brings the relief of the environment by shifting meat production to the factory and the associated argument for its product that this meat cannot transmit disease pathogens originating from animal husbandry (see Chriki & Hocquette, 2020).

However, this argument is certainly debatable. Not only is chicken meat subject to very strict health controls, which makes disease transmission unlikely, but we also know very little about the effects of cultivated meat on health. Currently, a fetal bovine serum (FBS) obtained from slaughtered calves is still essential for the nutrient solution. So far, cultivated chicken meat does not make the slaughter of animals unnecessary, but rather is a solution that shifts the ratio of individual killing to meat produced in favor of the animals. Accordingly, it is not the ultimate animal protection or even the interest in vegetarian nutrition, but the potential efficiency in meat production, which is why Singapore granted a license to Good Meat in 2020, which was further expanded in 2021 (see Business Wire, 2021). This permission to distribute the artificially produced meat is the first of its kind worldwide and at the same time a building block of the city-state to become independent of food imports in the long term. If the reports from Singapore available so far are correct, the proximity to the original is so convincing that no differences could be detected when consumed in a restaurant compared to chicken meat from a living chicken (see TRT World, 2020). Eat Just is thus a role model for a number of other companies, such as *Upside Food in*California, which have been producing cultivated meat in the USA with the most modern facility in the world since 2023. Cultivated meat is essential according to the ideas of this and many other companies to ensure the meat supply of the world population, which is still growing until the middle of the 21st century (see Upside Foods, 2023).

In summary, the goal of the brands presented here as examples cannot be imagined big enough—they are aiming for nothing less than saving the world. This is also the strategy in their branding: They highlight the indistinguishability between the respective product and the real meat derived from animals and emphasize the moral added value of the product. On the one hand, it is a topic in a whole series of videos produced either directly by the respective manufacturer or by others, in which people express their astonishment at having just consumed a meat alternative (see HiHo Kids., 2019). Children are particularly trusted to make an incorruptible judgment in this regard, but also restaurant visitors in Singapore up to public figures like *Bill Gates* testify surprise about the quality of the respective product (see Mark Rober, 2020). On the other hand, the customer should also know exactly that it is a meat that is beneficial to animal welfare and the environment, by the manufacturers highlighting this difference to meat in their branding and brand communication as a positive feature. Thus, brand names like *Just Food*, *Good Meat* and *Beyond Meat*, signal that the products go beyond the meat age and enable impeccable, healthy and morally justified nutrition.

The brand campaign of Beyond Meat relies on testimonials from consumers with multiethnic backgrounds, who report together with the famous rapper *Snoop Dogg* under the slogan "go beyond" how everyone can improve themselves and the world by switching to a vegan diet (see Beyond Meat. Why go Beyond, 2020). In other serial spots in the same warm tonality and underlaid with optimistically meaningful sounds, Beyond Ambassadors like the basketball players *Kyrie Irving* and *Chris Paul* describe their experiences and thoughts about a better world and good nutrition. It is not to be overlooked that all spots with phrases like "Making an impact", "Teaching people what I have learned", "Making a difference" and "Making a change" remind of a multitude of generic spots that advertise for social purposes, fascinating new technical products or for a different policy (see Dissolve, 2014). As an example, the spot "The Courage to Change" by Alexandria Ocasio-Cortez (2018) can be mentioned. Good Meat also follows a very similar strategy, somewhat more oriented towards didactic impulses, by reminding the web presence www.goodmeat.co of an environmental protection organization that presents its concern with all urgency. Through a high proportion of black areas and reduced typography, the visual design of the Good Meat website, like the packaging of Beyond Meat, conveys the feeling of high-quality products on the verge of luxury.

In summary, it becomes clear that these and many other manufacturers of meat alternatives primarily want to appeal to those relatively affluent consumers who are intellectually already prepared to switch to a better diet for the environment and animal welfare, but have not yet been ready for a change. These consumers are not supposed to be motivated by intellectual insight into the good, but by the fact that there is a possibility corresponding to their inclination to consume meat, which makes ethical action possible without special efforts or renunciation. In the marketing of Good Meat, it accordingly says: "Meat without deforestation. Meat without slaughter. Meat without limits." (Good Meat, 2022).

These brand strategies, however, seem to have little motivating effect on those who have so far unquestioningly viewed their own meat consumption positively. An impressively dramatic example is provided by the review of KFC Beyond Fried Chicken on the show *The Five* on the TV channel *Fox News* (Best of The Five, 2022). During a joint taste test, the five-member team of presenters expresses extensive outrage about the appearance, smell, and taste of the *Beyond Fried Chicken* and agree that this *Fake Meat* cannot be a satisfactory substitute for real chicken meat. One presenter demonstratively refuses to eat it, and another describes it as not even enjoyable for a dog. In addition to these outbursts, the statement made by the designated enfant terrible *Greg Gutfeld* is noteworthy, suggesting that we generally appreciate our food less if the act of killing did not precede consumption. This maliciously formulated, but not incorrect, interjection is as worth considering as the shyly rejecting reaction of his colleagues after a brief moment of shock.

Upon closer examination, this masterpiece of conservative infotainment accurately reflects the ambivalent symbolic significance that meat consumption has in human culture. The consequences of consuming animals for the development of human self-image cannot be overstated. Following the considerations of *Roberto Calasso*, we must understand hunting and thus the availability of fresh meat as a relatively late achievement, with which man has risen from being a scavenger to the dominant position over nature that we take for granted (cf. Calasso, 2020, pos. 2170). This long-standing association of superiority with male physical strength is reflected today, for example, in the slogan "Man, that's a sausage" of the Bruzzler brand by *Wiesenhof* (2023). In its blunt way, this slogan also refers to the archaic relationship to nutrition, which *Sigmund Freud*, among others, describes in his psychology of religion as the magical function of meat consumption (cf. Freud, 1922, p. 133 ff.). From early totemism to the Eucharist and beyond, the magic described by Freud is plausible, that the powers of an animal are transferred to the human being through its consumption. At the same time, Freud, like Calasso later, points to the ambivalent feeling of guilt that has always accompanied the killing of an animal due to its kinship with the animal as a sentient being. Calasso sees this feeling as the deeper reason for both the religious rules of slaughter, as they exist in Judaism and Islam, and the modern regulations for this process. He finds it remarkable that these rules, then as now, are intended to protect not the animal, but the perpetrator from the act of killing:

> "As far as secular society is concerned, there is the rule that the animal should be stunned before it is killed. This is said to be done to shorten and alleviate its suffering. But the animal suffers most before it is killed. Tortured, forced, goaded, so that it does not resist and does not cause time losses. The stunning is more likely to stun the one who kills than the one who is killed. It is a euphemization of death. It is supposed to convince the one who kills that he is killing an almost already dead being." (Calasso, 2020, pos. 2136).

Understood in this way, meat consumption is associated with an ambivalence between an act of killing the animal that testifies to dominance and, at the same time, a feeling of shame for this act.

In this context, the analysis by *Norbert Elias* is finally revealing, that the meat served on the table is increasingly less associated with killing and dismembering due to shame about the violence against the animal as the civilizing process progresses:

> "The dismembering itself does not disappear, since the animal must be dismembered if one wants to eat it. But what has become embarrassing is moved behind the scenes of social life. Specialists take care of it in the shop or in the kitchen. It will be shown again and again how characteristic this figure of segregating, this 'moving behind the scenes' of what has become embarrassing is for the whole process of what we call 'civilization'." (Elias, 1981, p. 254f.).

Due to this shame that also affects our society, the act of killing a sentient being is obscured in the ongoing process of civilization, without, however, diminishing the awareness of consuming an animal. The juicy steak is therefore indeed associated with a feeling of dominance over the strong ox, whose strength and potency one incorporates, bypassing the guilt-ridden process of killing a living being. This insight applies equally to all less high-quality forms of meat such as kebabs, cheeseburgers, and Chicken McNuggets, which democratize the symbolic dominance reserved for the upper classes. In this context, the standardized formed meat of the fast food industry is transformed into a standardized product that creates the greatest possible distance to the killing, dismembering, and even the consumption of real animal meat, yet does not completely deny its origin. According to this understanding, even civilized meat eaters like the host team of The Five on Fox News still find themselves in the ambivalent situation of wanting their meat, including the symbolic meaning of dominance, in agreement with the act of killing, without having to confront their own shame. This becomes even clearer in that in this case it is about *Chicken Nuggets*, which are not to be replaced by a plant-based product. Anyone who equates such industrially manufactured products with meat in its natural form seems to be primarily concerned with the killing of animals as a distinguishing feature. For this significant group of consumers, the slogan often used by progressive circles, "Taking the animal out of the food equation" (cf. Conningham, 2021), represents a loss calculation that cannot be offset by the similar consistency or taste of substitute products like *Beyond Meat*. Not least because the social recognition that progressive consumers experience within their peer group through the consumption of the products is not given to them. On the contrary, for this group of consumers, the consumption of real animals is part of a self-image that feels threatened by the technically sophisticated products of modern food production. From their perspective, we must imagine the modern reincarnations of the villain Jacques Trikatell as the CEOs of the aforementioned brands.

Certainly, the development of alternative meat products is still in its early stages, and it is therefore understandable that the products are tailored to those *early adopters* who can better put their idealism into practice with the products of Beyond Meat, Just Food, and other manufacturers. However, this cannot remain the case for long if the aim is to differently shape a significant part of the diet that is still based on meat in the future. With regard to branding, manufacturers should therefore primarily realize that educational measures will not be successful. Nobody changes their eating habits out of mere insight. Just as the added value of the brands Beyond Meat and Good Meat lies in enabling the progressive clientele to have a diet that corresponds to their ideas and inclinations without great effort, the conservative consumer will not be deterred from his preferences by the intellectual insights of other people. Even if it should correspond to the conviction and the feeling of life of the advertisers themselves, a large part of the broad mass will not be motivated to change their habits with an approach based on environmental protection, technology, and the magic of start-ups. It is rather to be assumed that this part of the population will continue to prefer meat consumption. It therefore seems obvious that a communication of meat substitute products that is less based on morality and technology and more on classic attributes of meat is more promising to them. Ideally, one would then be dealing with flawlessly tasty burgers, chicken nuggets, sizzlers, etc. beyond the classic production of meat, whose artificial production is so insignificant for the end consumer that it disappears in the small print.

References

@justegg. (1 April 2021). Tweet. https://twitter.com/justegg/status/1377674698985668609. Accessed 20 Dec. 2023.

Andrews, J. (29 July 2019). Beyond Meat's Chicken Came First, and It Was a Failure. Wall Street and Investors Don't Care. CNBC. https://www.cnbc.com/2019/07/29/beyond-meats-chicken-came-first-and-it-was-a-failure.html. Accessed 20 Dec. 2023.

Best of The Five. (6 January 2022). Would You Try KFC's Beyond Fried Chicken? https://www.youtube.com/watch?v=5NPMRzJjMmg. Accessed 20 Dec. 2023.

Beyond Meat. (21 May 2020). Why Go Beyond. https://www.youtube.com/watch?v=k7B3eF3oLy0. Accessed 23 Dec. 2023.

Beyond Meat. (2023a). Ingredients. https://www.beyondmeat.com/en-US/about/our-ingredients/. Accessed 23 Dec. 2023.

Beyond Meat. (2023b). Plant-based meat products. https://www.beyondmeat.com/en-US/products/.

Business Wire. (15 December 2021). GOOD Meat Granted Regulatory Approval for New Chicken Products in Singapore as Company Plans for Larger-Scale Production. https://www.businesswire.com/news/home/20211215006131/en/GOOD-Meat-Granted-Regulatory-Approval-for-New-Chicken-Products-in-Singapore-as-Company-Plans-for-Larger-Scale-Production. Accessed 23 Dec. 2023.

Calasso, R. (2020). *Der Himmlische Jäger* (Kindle). Suhrkamp Verlag.

Chriki, S., & Hocquette, J.-F. (2020). The Myth of Cultured Meat: A Review. Frontiers in nutrition, *7*, 7. https://doi.org/10.3389/fnut.2020.00007.

CNBC International. (2021). Eat Just: The Multibillion-Dollar Company Selling Lab-Grown Chicken Meat. https://www.youtube.com/watch?v=xeZ_o_eqt38. Accessed 20 Dec. 2023.

Conningham. C. (1 April 2021). A New Generation of Innovators Create the Future of Meat. https://antagonist.co/where-is-the-heme-on-the-future-of-vegan-meat/. Accessed 20 Dec. 2023.

Dissolve. (2014). This Is a Generic Brand Video. https://www.youtube.com/watch?v=2YBtspm8j8M. Accessed 20 Dec. 2023.

Elias, N. (1981). *Über den Prozeß der Zivilisation: Soziogenetische und psychogenetische Untersuchungen* (Vol. 1): Wandlungen des Verhaltens in den weltlichen Oberschichten des Abendlandes. Suhrkamp.

Freud, S. (1922). *Totem und Tabu. Einige Übereinstimmungen im Seelenleben der Wilden und der Neurotiker*. Leipzig, Wien, Zürich: Internationaler Psychoanalytischer Verlag.

Good Meat. (2022). Good Meat. The Future of Meat. https://goodmeat.co. Accessed 20 Dec. 2023.

Goy, I. (2007). *Immanuel Kant über das moralische Gefühl der Achtung*. Zeitschrift für philosophische Forschung, *61*(3), 337–360, [p. 349]. http://www.jstor.org/stable/20484686. Accessed 17 May 2023.

HiHo Kids. (9 July 2019). Kids Try Beyond and Impossible Burgers. https://www.youtube.com/watch?v=FqGI3iMX_co. Accessed 20 Dec. 2023.

Hume, D. (1978). *A treatise of human nature*, in: L. A. Selby-Bigge & P. H. Nidditch (Eds.), A treatise of human nature (2nd edn.). Clarendon Press. (Originalwerk veröffentlicht 1739–1740).

Just Egg. (2023). https://www.ju.st. Accessed 20 Dec. 2023.

Kant, I., (1785). Grundlegung zur Metaphysik der Sitten. In I. Kant & (1900ff) G. Schriften. (Eds.), Bd. 1–22, *Preussische Akademie der Wissenschaften*, Bd. 23 *Deutsche Akademie der Wissenschaften zu Berlin*, ab Bd. 24, *Akademie der Wissenschaften zu Göttingen*. Bd. 4.

Leenaert, T. (9 February 2014). On Meat Wating and Rationality: Richard Dawkins and Sam Harris. In *The Vegan Strategist*. https://veganstrategist.org/2014/02/09/on-meat-eating-and-rationality-richard-dawkins-and-sam-harris/. Accessed 20 Dec. 2023.

Lucas, A., & Rogers, K. (1 April 2022). KFC to Launch Plant-based Fried Chicken Made with Beyond Meat Nationwide. https://www.cnbc.com/2022/01/04/kfc-to-launch-meatless-fried-chicken-made-with-beyond-meat-nationwide.html. Accessed 20 Dec. 2023.

Market Watch. (5 May 2019), Beyond Meat Ssoars 163 % in Biggest-popping U. S. IPO Since 2000. https://www.marketwatch.com/story/beyond-meat-soars-163-in-biggest-popping-us-ipo-since-2000-2019-05-02. Accessed 20 Dec. 2023.

Ocasio-Cortez, A. (30 May 2018). The courage to change|Alexandria Ocasio-Cortez. https://www.youtube.com/watch?v=rq3QXIVR0bs. Accessed 20 Dec. 2023.

Parker, A. (9 August 2016). Donald Trump's diet: He'll have fries with that. https://www.nytimes.com/2016/08/09/us/politics/donald-trump-diet.html. Accessed 20 Dec. 2023.

Piazza, J., Ruby, M. B., Loughnan, S., Luong, M., Kulik, J., Watkins, H. M., & Seigerman, M. (2015). *Rationalizing meat consumption. The 4Ns. Appetite, 91*, 114–128. https://doi.org/10.1016/j.appet.2015.04.011. Epub 2015 Apr. 9. PMID: 25865663.

Recki, B. (2006). *Die Vernunft, ihre Natur, ihr Gefühl und der Fortschritt. Aufsätze zu Immanuel Kant*. Paderborn: Mentis.

Ried, K. (31 January 2019). Awareness-Maßnahme: Fischer Appelt: Kuh killt in Peta-Kampagne in: Werben & Verkaufen. https://www.wuv.de/agenturen/fischer_appelt_kuh_killt_in_peta_kampagne. Accessed 20 Dec. 2023.

Rober, M. (13 February 2020). Feeding Bill Gates a Fake Burger (to Save the World). https://www.youtube.com/watch?v=-k-V3ESHcfA. Accessed 20 Dec. 2023.

TRT World. (22 December 2020). Singapore First Country to Approve Sale of Lab-Grown Chicken. https://www.youtube.com/watch?v=RVWU9rbylhc. Accessed 20 Dec. 2023. Accessed 11 May 2023.

UPSIDE Foods. (2023). Progress for People, Animals, and Planet. https://upsidefoods.com/progress. Accessed 20 Dec. 2023.

WIESENHOF Bruzzzler. (2023). WIESENHOF Bruzzzler: Die Geschichte der Kult-Bratwurst. https://www.wiesenhof-bruzzzler.de/geschichte/. Accessed 20 Dec. 2023.

Yu, D. (25 June 2021). Eat Just Mulls $3 Billion IPO to Eventually Make Cruelty-Free Food Mainstream. Forbes. https://www.forbes.com/sites/douglasyu/2021/06/25/eat-just-mulls-3-billion-ipo-to-eventually-make-cruelty-free-food-mainstream/. Accessed 20 Dec. 2023.

Zidi, C. (1976). *L'Aile ou la Cuisse*. Christian Fechner Produktion.

9

Boy London: The Logo is the Brand

Abstract Although brands without a visual identity are hardly conceivable, the status of logos is not uncontested. Logos are probably necessary, but should not be equated with the actual brand. In light of this, the question arises as to what role logos actually play and how one should imagine the existence of a brand beyond its visual representation through these symbols. Using the example of the Boy London brand, both the difference between the function of a logo as a sign and as a symbol, as well as the circumstance that we can indeed equate brands with their logo under certain conditions, can be demonstrated.

A common theme in introductions to brand design and brand management is the assertion that a brand is not exhausted in a logo. Anyone who refers to a pictorial and word mark as a brand in itself has not understood that brands are something other than stylized graphics and catchy names. This reservation is vividly brought to the point in an illustration by *Marty Neumeier* that refers to the famous painting *La Trahison des Images* (1929) by *René Magritte* and shows a Nike logo in the style of the painting with the subtitle "Ceci n'est pas une brand" (Neumeier, 2005, p. 10). The adaptation of the artwork is intended to show that, just as the image of a pipe is not a real pipe, we must not confuse a logo with the brand itself. In further elaborations on the picture, it is explained that the brand is not the logo, a corporate design system, or the product, but "a person's gut feeling" (ibid., p. 11) about a branded product, service, or organization.

As creative as the reference to Magritte and as practical as the hint to the feeling may initially appear, closer examination reveals inconsistencies that in turn provide insight into the actual relationship between brand and logo. For this, let's first look at the original artwork by Magritte. It is the generally accepted punchline of this surrealist work that in contrast to a painted pipe on a work of art, one can ascertain in the face of an actual pipe: "Look here, this is a real pipe—ceci es une pipe!" The standard interpretation is therefore that Magritte in his painting points out the difference between real and merely imagined objects: A painted pipe is not a real pipe.

The illustration with the Nike logo also emphasizes this same difference. However, one can also realize that the relationship between image and real logo is much more problematic here, because Nike is not an object like a table or a pipe. In line with the brand as an intangible asset of a company, one cannot divert one's gaze from the painted Nike logo and point to the brand as a concrete object. Even someone who holds a Nike sneaker in their hands is not dealing with the brand as an object, but with something that refers to the brand.

In light of this, if we ask ourselves whether the reference to the gut feeling as the actual brand can solve the problem, it is undisputed that brands trigger emotions. However, one can also realize that feelings are usually not about the felt thing itself. Rather, as the *emotional intentionalism* according to *Franz Brentano* describes, it is a form of reference to an object different from the feeling (cf. Brentano, 1874/1982). We feel the pain of an injury, rejoice in our own success, and feel discomfort in the presence of an unsympathetic person, meaning something different from our feeling. Just as we can take our inner states in countless other cases as meaningful indications for certain facts different from them, a certain gut feeling can thus be interpreted as a reliable sign of dealing with a brand. However, the fact that this feeling in the pit of the stomach is the place where we feel our relationship to a brand does not make it the brand itself, just as pain is not the injury itself.

Since the brand is neither a feeling nor a concrete object, the only remaining option is to define it as an abstract object, as described by *Wolfgang Künne*. According to his findings, abstract objects are those objects that do not exist materially or as mental states, but to which we can refer with words or symbols (cf. Künne, 1983/2007). In this definition, he includes relationships and propositions, but also natural kinds and types. Against this background, one could state that brands are abstract objects in the sense of types that subsume certain objects—branded articles—under them. Without making this categorical difference between an abstract object and a feeling clear, Marty Neumeier then formulates it in such a way that a brand is "a kind of platonic idea—a concept to identify a specific class of things." (Neumeier, 2006, p. 12). However, to establish this means that brands are indeed something other than the previously apostrophized "gut feelings", namely *abstract objects* to which these feelings refer.

Bearing this in mind, we can understand the illustration referring to Magritte as a hint as to how logos, while not being brands *per se*, cannot be separated from them. To clarify this, we can go back to the beginning and first realize that we usually equate the visual impression of all images with their object. In this undisturbed state, the depiction of the Nike logo is perceived as the brand *Nike* just as we call the image of a pipe a *pipe*. Only in a distance caused by a disturbance, as generated by the subtitle "Ceci n´est pas une brand", do we become aware of the difference between the image and its object. It is important to note that as viewers, before we consider the being of brands, we would probably first notice that a Nike logo painted by an artist is not the real logo of this brand. Only in a second step does the composition make us think about the relationship of this logo to its object. It is not even certain that the image necessarily makes us think about the ontological status of brands. It can just as well stimulate thinking about the relationship between copy and original—the artistic interpretation of a logo is not authentic in the same sense as the actual brand emblem. If we equate it with the original or apply the subtitle "Ceci n'est pas une brand" as a comment to the original logo, as we find it in hundreds of thousands of executions on products, uniforms of service employees or other brand touchpoints, it is obvious that the comment, that we are not dealing with a brand, does not directly suggest thoughts about the actual being of a brand. Rather, it raises doubts about dealing with a real brand in the sense of an original or authentic brand product.

Worth mentioning in this context is *Gernot Böhme's* view of Magritte's work, who points out that the subtitle is to be understood in the sense of an advertisement that does not highlight the deficit of the image, but the special feature of the depicted brand product compared to generic products. *Ceci n'est pas une pipe* in this reading does not refer to the ontological status of images, but describes the special position of the depicted brand product emphasized in advertising, for example in the sense of the slogan: "This is not a pipe, but a Stanwell." (Böhme, 1995).

However, the opposite could also be conceivable, namely that this is not a *real* pipe, because it is not the brand product, but a mere copy. Just as the subtitle "Ceci n´est pas une pipe" on a real pipe would suggest a dummy or at least not the desirable specimen of a real pipe, in the case of a real logo with the handwritten subtitle "Ceci n'est pas une brand", we would initially assume a kind of brand dummy. Such brand dummies can include fakes of established brands on the one hand. On the other hand, logos are also to be understood as brand dummies that only superficially represent a real brand. These include, for example, the *Stay-Puft Marshmallow Man* from Ivan Reitman's *Ghostbusters* (1984) or the ACME lettering used by *Warner Brothers*, which has appeared in their cartoons as a placeholder for fictional brand manufacturers since the 1920s. But also many of those logos that pretend to stand for products from independent manufacturers as *Private-Label-Brands* in the range of stationary and online retailers can be described as brand dummies. In this regard, one can also speak of a brand dummy whenever a logo looking like a traditional producer is designed and then mounted on products from a generic source. These are the Bohemian villages of branding, behind whose facade there is no identifiable producer with its own history and special claim. The boundary between mere illustration of products and actual brands is fluid. Some Private Label Brands have actually developed a life of their own, which makes them appear as authentic brands, whereas others remain mere images without reference to an abstract object. However, the distinction can be made less by definite rational criteria than it is actually a matter of gut feeling to sense the respective difference between a brand logo as a symbol and as a mere illustration.

Returning to the illustration of the Nike logo made in the style of Magritte, it is also possible to understand this logo in the first step in the sense of a brand dummy. This leads in the second step to the consideration that we are not dealing with a brand here because the merely copied logo does not symbolically represent the abstract object of the Nike brand. In view of this, one can understand the punchline of the adaptation of Magritte as referring to the actual being of the brand as an abstract object that always also requires a symbolization. Even if the logo is not the brand itself, it is recognized that a brand is an abstract object that relies on a symbolic reference point for emotional and intellectual associations. With *Hans Domizlaff's* idea of a brand personality, we can also describe this as the logo being an essential part of the "face of the brand" (Domizlaff, 1939/2005, p. 190) and indispensable for its expression. It is therefore just as wrong to call a logo a brand as to claim that a brand could do without a visual anchor in reality.

Although brands are unimaginable without this visual symbolic expression, the adaptation of Magritte's image *La Trahison des Images* also shows the particular skepticism often expressed towards logos. In addition to the relative simplicity with which any logos can be mounted on objects and thus brand dummies can be fabricated, it also seems to be rooted in the relative arbitrariness of their design. Therefore, it is clear that a brand is not just a logo, because there is no absolute necessity for a particular design to belong to a particular brand. The professional design of a logo probably includes certain preferences, inspirations, professional experiences, and empirical studies. However, this knowledge alone does not make a logo a symbol that could decide the existence or non-existence of a particular brand.

In fact, this only describes the function of logos as signs, as Ernst Cassirer's differentiation between signals or signs on the one hand and symbols on the other hand illustrates:

> "Symbols—in the proper sense of this term—cannot be reduced to mere signals. Signals and symbols belong to two different universes of discourse: a signal is a part of the physical world of being; a symbol is a part of the human world of meaning. Signals are 'operators'; symbols are 'designators'." (Cassirer, 1944/1967, p. 32).

Regarding the obvious objection that a signal always also has a specific meaning, Cassirer emphasizes its necessary anchoring in the physical world: "Signals, even when understood and used as such, have nevertheless a sort of physical or substantial being; symbols have only a functional value." (Ibid.). Signs only function against the background of immediate events, in whose context they signal something, whereas symbols are fundamentally detached from specific situations because they refer to a horizon of meaning lying outside spatial boundaries. Pointing out the appropriate graphic design of a logo can therefore explain a sign-like quality suitable for the particular brand, but does not justify its function as a meaningful symbol. It is therefore justified and helpful if a logo suggests appropriate associations about the function of a brand; however, it is not a necessary requirement for a brand logo to be a well-functioning signal or sign.

Further insight into this relationship is provided by the language theory of *Ferdinand Saussure,* who points out that language consists of two components (Saussure, 1916). He calls the linguistic expression the *Signifiant* and the conceptual content the *Signifié* and emphasizes that there is no natural connection between these two components. Instead, the relationship between Signifiant and Signifié is arbitrary, meaning there is no inherent reason why a particular word as Signifiant should be associated with a particular concept as the Signifié. The necessity of the connection only arises with the conventions of language use that are established in use. Analogously, one can imagine a logo as a Signifiant that is relatively arbitrarily assigned to a Signifié, but then becomes necessary forms of expression in conventional use. No matter how creative and appropriate a particular logo design may be in its form as a sign, it is not absolutely mandatory in its form, and it only gains its symbolic meaning through conventional handling. Not the shape itself, but use and familiarity can give the logo, which is by no means interchangeable, its quite magical symbolic meaning as an embodiment of a brand. The magic now consists in the fact that we perceive the logo as a quasi-animated object and identify it as the face of the brand with its being.

Brand logos are only one category within the network of infinitely many symbols into which our world is structured and whose symbolism only becomes apparent to us as such in the distance. Thus, we can relate Magritte's subtitle to any abstract and concrete objects and become aware of the difference between symbol, convention, and object from the resulting reflection distance. In a broader form, this distance is implemented in *iconoclastic* movements that aim to break up the conventional effect of symbols by destroying them. We can also understand the punk movement that emerged in the 1970s as a variant of iconoclastic distancing. Traditional norms and symbols are negated, provocatively reinterpreted, and partly turned into their opposite to escape the stuffiness of the petty-bourgeois milieu. Despite the moral claim with which this youth movement confronts the adapted average existence, the provocation reaches its dubious climax in the affirmative reference to the symbols of absolute evil. It is the time when *David Bowie*, openly flirting with fascism, makes a name for himself as the *Thin White Duke* and representatives of the punk scene, most notably *Vivian Westwood*, openly display Nazi symbols. These are shown not to pay homage to the uniform oppression of a contemptuous system, but to cause the greatest possible shock. If one wanted to gain something from this in retrospect, then that these gestures of the rebellious-disillusioned youth have fully explored the power of aesthetic seduction and the power of symbols through their distancing shift.

The creation of the brand *Boy London* in 1976 falls into this melange of time, which can be understood as a direct response to the demand for new, contemporary fashion labels that opened up with the punk movement. The founders benefited from their long-standing experience in managing the scene boutique ACME Attractions when they opened the eponymous store at 153 King's Road. Their illustrious clientele included The Clash, Sex Pistols, Chrissie Hynde, Patti Smith, Deborah Harry, and Bob Marley. The knack for developing appropriate marketing for a target group that perceives itself as outside the societal grid, which was already evident here, continues in the staging of the Boy London brand. Distance from the mainstream is primarily established by the logo, which was designed by *Peter Christopherson,* creator of the iconic album cover for *Pink Floyd's* album *The Dark Side of the Moon* (1973) (cf. Boy London, 2023b). It features a stylized eagle spreading its wings, similar to the party eagle of the NSDAP or the later *Reich's eagle* but facing in the opposite direction (cf. Koop, 2012, p. 46 ff.). Besides finer graphic differences, the striking difference to the fashion brand's logo is that where the National Socialist eagle holds a closed wreath of oak leaves around a swastika in its claws, the circular O of the brand name, set in capital letters of a sans-serif linear antiqua, stands.

From Saussure's semiotic perspective, the effect of the logo is based on the use of the same Signifiant for completely different, even opposing Signifié. In Cassirer's terminology, this would be two different symbols associated with the same sign, and Künne would speak of two almost identical symbols referring to different abstract objects. However, these abstract objects do not exist completely independently of each other due to their specific opposition. The stimulus emanating from the fashion brand lies rather in the subversive gesture of having transformed an evil sign into a progressive symbol. It structurally follows the same distancing and reinterpretation as was far less spectacularly the case with the use of the ACME brand dummy for a fashion store. The boutique, whose brand name embodies an ironic distancing from the brand world, is contrasted with a fashion label whose logo is based on the ironic use of a Nazi symbol. Both are based on the strategy of *Socratic irony* extensively discussed by *Sören Kierkegaard,* which is the freedom to separate inner attitude from external conventions (cf. Kierkegaard, 1841/2019). Anyone who wears *Boy London* shows their affiliation with the subculture by not committing to the conventions of societal ostracism of certain symbols and being free to handle even potentially dangerous aesthetic variants of the symbolic.

The avant-garde image resulting from this has been helped by celebrities such as *Andy Warhol* and *Madonna* in the 1980s, just as the brand attracts celebrities like *Lady Gaga* and *Rihanna* today. As a result, Boy London has never played a role in the right-wing scene in the same way as other English fashion labels. Precisely because the symbol is so overt and the brand ambassadors are so clearly attributable to the progressive mainstream, the image of the travesty of the burdened sign overlays the appeal of the logo for neo-Nazis. The paradox is that the loss of appeal for right-wing radicals is a result of the fact that the logo is actually the reinterpreted National Socialist symbol of power. If it were an eagle similar to, but recognizably different from, the Nazi symbol, the ironic gesture would not be possible in the same way. Then it would at least be conceivable that the brand, similar to the fashion label *Londsdale*, would be co-opted by neo-Nazis due to coincidental similarities with fascist codes. (The problem with the Londsdale brand is that only the letters NSDA are visible from the logo printed on the front of their sweaters when a (bomber) jacket is open, which can be misused as a cipher. The brand counters this problem with proactive engagement against racism and fascism).

This observation makes it clear that it is difficult to understand when Boy London retreats, in the face of criticism of the use of the burdened symbol, to never having referred to the Third Reich and always to the similarly designed eagle of the Roman Empire (cf. EUIPO, 2021; Thaidigsmann, 2021). Even if one wanted to follow this implausible argument in the light of the analysis presented here, the criticism of the brand's appearance, especially from the Jewish side, should be sufficient to completely abandon the logo. The confirmation of the deletion of the emblematic eagle as a trademark by the *European Intellectual Property Office* (EUIPO, 2021) has expressed this demand for distancing from the burdened symbol in Europe, but has not achieved its actual goal. Today, the eagle is indeed recognizably absent from the corporate design on the official website www.boy-london.com (cf. Boy London, 2023a). However, the symbol is still found as a graphic element on many garments of the so-called Heritage Collection (cf. Boy London, 2023c). With this in mind, it can be assumed that many consumers still identify it as a common logo of the brand, especially since it appears on the international websites registered in Korea *en.boylondoninternational.com* (cf. Boy London International, 2023) and the same address with *cn.* (cf. Boy London CN, 2023) as a prefix still in the sense of a brand logo in the web interface and on most garments. Apart from the problem of international jurisdiction that emerges here, this also reveals something fundamental about the importance of logos for brands. The fact that one does not want to completely separate from this burdened sign despite strong criticism not only shows the importance of the brand's own symbol for Boy London. It also points to how closely we should imagine the relationship between brands and their logos in general.

Another twist in the discourse about Boy London and the importance of logos for brands in general can be seen in the fact that the brand has been extremely successful in Asia, especially in the Chinese market, in the last decade. After settling long-standing trademark disputes with Chinese copycats of their brand name and eagle symbol, Boy London gained a mainstream character in China in the early 2020s that can only astonish Western observers (cf. Rapp, 2019). Even though it made headlines for some time in the early 2010s, most Chinese are completely unaware of the connection between the logo and Germany's recent history. Without causing much fuss, Boy London stores with the eagle logo above the entrance area can therefore be found quite naturally in the countless shopping malls of the country, alongside the ubiquitous Adidas, Nike, and Uniqlo stores. With this generally innocent view of the guilt-laden sign, however, the reflexively ironic meaning of the brand is also lost. Its perception here rather goes hand in hand with a quite general idea of strength, without the eagle being associated with specific historical models. One could therefore argue that the symbol here no longer refers to the same abstract object as elsewhere. In this sense, Boy London in China can be taken as an example of a brand that is not a brand dummy, but where the brand and logo seem to be so close together that a variation of Magritte's *La Trahison des Images* might raise the question of the original, but not the problem of the status of logos. Here, the opposite of what the statement insinuating in relation to Magritte denies applies: "Je suis un logo, je suis une brand." "I am a logo, I am a brand."

References

Böhme, G. (1995). *Das ist doch eine Pfeife. Über Kunst und Werbung bei Magritte*. In: Kunst Forum Bd. 125 (pp. 166–177). https://www.kunstforum.de/artikel/das-ist-doch-eine-pfeife/. Accessed 20 Dec. 2023.
Boy London. (2023a). https://www.boy-london.com. Accessed 20 Dec. 2023.
Boy London. (2023b). Press. https://www.boy-london.com/pages/press. Accessed 20 Dec. 2023.
Boy London. (2023c). Mens clothes. https://www.boy-london.com/collections/men. Accessed 20 Dec. 2023.
Boy London CN. (2023). https://cn.boylondoninternational.com. Accessed 20 Dec. 2023.
Boy London International. (2023). https://en.boylondoninternational.com/index.html. Accessed 20 Dec. 2023.
Brentano, F. (1982). *Psychologie vom empirischen Standpunkt*. Felix Meiner Verlag. (Originalwerk veröffentlicht 1874).
Cassirer, E. (1967). *An Essay on Man: An Introduction to a Philosophy of Human Culture*. Yale University Press. (Originalwerk veröffentlicht 1944).
Domizlaff, H. (2005). *Die Gewinnung des öffentlichen Vertrauens*. Marketing Journal. Gesellschaft für angewandtes Marketing mbH (Originalwerk veröffentlicht 1939).

EUIPO. (23 April 2021). Case R 0459/2020-5. https://euipo.europa.eu/eSearch-CLW/#key/trademark/APL_20210423_R0459_2020-5_011708773. Accessed 20 Jan. 2024.

Kierkegaard, S. (2019). *Über den Begriff der Ironie: Mit ständiger Rücksicht auf Sokrates.* Reprint der Edition von 1929.De Gruyter. (Originalwerk veröffentlicht 1841).

Koop, A. (2012). *NSCI- Das visuelle Erscheinungsbild der Nationalsozialisten 1920–1945.* Verlag Hermann Schmidt.

Künne, W. (2007), *Abstrakte Gegenstände. Semantik und Ontologie.*(2., um einen Anhang erweiterte Aufl.) Vittorio Klostermann (Originalwerk veröffentlicht 1983).

Neumeier, M. (2006). The Brand Gap: How to Bridge the Distance Between Business Strategy and Design. New Riders.

Pink Floyd (1973). The Dark Side of the Moon. [Album]. Capitol.

Rapp, J. (28 April 2019). How UK streetwear brand boy London beat China's copycats and is finally booming in the country. *South China Morning Post.* https://www.scmp.com/lifestyle/fashion-beauty/article/3007775/how-uk-streetwear-brand-boy-london-beat-chinas-copycats. Accessed 20 Dec. 2023.

Saussure, F. de (1916). *Cours de linguistique générale* [Grundfragen der allgemeinen Sprachwissenschaft]. Payot.

Thaidigsmann, M. (11 May 2021). Sittenwidrig: »NSDAP-Adler« keine EU-Marke. https://www.juedische-allgemeine.de/politik/sittenwidrig-nsdap-adler-keine-eingetragene-eu-marke/. Accessed 20 Dec. 2023.

10

Bored Apes & Co: NFTs and Art as a Brand

Abstract The migration of art into the digital sphere has entered public consciousness with the success of NFTs in recent years. However, the status of these digital originals in contrast to artworks in traditional media is still unclear. Looking at commercially successful NFT projects, it could be said that NFT art explores the boundary of art by distinguishing itself primarily through its monetary value and relying heavily on brand building.

In the last novel of the remarkable trilogy *The Three Body Problem* by Chinese science fiction author *Liu Cixin* (2019), the life-weary, shy-nerdy astrophysicist *Tianming* seeks a particularly unusual gift for a romantically unattainable former classmate. He eventually finds it in the fictional UNESCO project *Stars Our Destination*, with which the international authority ventures into the vicinity of shady business dealings. It is a fundraiser through which they sell *certified property* of distant stars. Deeply moved by his romantic feelings, Tianming invests his entire, not so small fortune in a star that is just affordable for him, which, despite the unreachable distance of 285.5 light years, can be seen from Earth under favorable conditions. Unfortunately, the money is not enough for a celestial body closer to Earth, which may be located in the center of a planetary system.

Had Liu Cixin written his novel a decade later, the transaction might have been handled via the internet portal *opensea.com*, where the sad hero could have invested his entire fortune just as easily in a *certificate* for an object that is completely virtual from his standpoint. The advantage for the novelist in this variant would be that he would not have to invent this detail of his narrative. Opensea.com sells digital NFT artworks that adorn a living room as little as a distant star and that anyone with a browser can enjoy just as easily as anyone can look into the night sky. Moreover, it would have been easy for the author to embed the unexpected increase in the value of the gift, which is important in his narrative, into a realistic scenario. Of course, he would have to design his time horizon differently. While the acquisition of the foreign star in the novel only leads to great wealth after centuries, the NFT market already jumped by 21,350% in 2021, bringing investors exorbitant profits worth more than $5 billion (Nonfungible & L'Atelier, 2021, p. 34).

Indeed, the great success of digital certificates for artworks, which neither materialize nor correspond to the canon of previous high-priced visual art, leaves one somewhat puzzled. At the same time, these digital works are fascinating because we seem to observe an innovation in visual art that we have not experienced for a good century. In this understanding, NFTs are an epochal renewal in art, continuing the change that took place in the 20th century in the sense that not only very mundane material, but also equally ordinary immaterial objects can be "art".

This development begins with *Marcel Duchamp* submitting the artwork *Fountain* under the pseudonym *Richard Mutt* for an exhibition of the *Society of Independent Artist* in New York in April 1917, which is a urinal purchased in a store, dated and signed. In the immediate discussion that followed, initiated by the artist himself, about whether any and in principle interchangeable object can be a work of art, Duchamp's defenders argue that it is solely up to the artist's decision from which material he creates a work and thus declares it to be a work of art (cf. Roche et al., 1917, pp. 4 ff.). Decades later, the philosopher *Arthur Danto* describes the epochal innovation that emanates from Duchamp's works:

> "And in my own investigations into the philosophy of art, I have benefited immensely from Duchamp's discovery that nothing the eye can reveal will arbitrate the difference between a work of art and a mere real thing which resembles it in every outward particular. So any proposed distinction based upon perceptual differences, even in the visual arts, will have proved, as with the linnaean system in botany, to be artificial, however useful in practice." (Danto, 1986, p. 135).

Danto suggests with the emphasis on the discovery of certain relationships by the artist that Duchamp, with his readymades, stumbled upon a connection that has always been latent in reality, just as the first wheel was a discovery that goes beyond the immediate invention. He also implies that real progress and epochal discoveries can take place not only in technical areas, but also in the development of culture.

This view is already represented by *G.W.F. Hegel*, who believes that this development is accompanied, among other things, by an already reached *end of art*. Hegel's assumption is that culture has reached the end of the development of certain social structures when they are so mature that they serve as ideal instruments for solving their own intracultural problems (cf. Jaeschke, 2010, p. 416 ff.). The *end* of something thus does not mean at all that it disappears, but rather that it is fully matured and thus designed for permanence. The *end of history* anticipated by Hegel, most recently prominently prophesied with the historical analysis of *Francis Fukuyama*, would therefore be reached when the major questions of historical-cultural development are permanently clarified in practice—"(…) there would be no further progress in the development of underlying principles and institutions, because all of the really big questions had been settled." (Fukuyama, 1992).

Long before this probably still long outstanding state, the institution of art experiences its mature peak in the representation of religious content in the culture of ancient Greece shaped by religion and myth, according to Hegel's assumption. However, since the artistic representation cannot move beyond the realm of representations, it has also reached the end point of its development. It exceeds the possibilities of artistic representations to go beyond what is just pictorially representable and to represent the conceptual contents of scientifically enlightened consciousness appropriately, while standing at the height of advancing intellectual development. At the same time, the conceptually formed consciousness can no longer be impressed in the same way by the emotionally colored representations of visual art. Hegel illustrates this impression with the often quoted image that we can be deeply impressed by the Greek god images and Christian-religious motifs, but our knee does not bend before them anymore due to our enlightened consciousness:

> "No matter how excellent we find the Greek god images, and God the Father, Christ, Mary, no matter how worthy and perfectly represented, it doesn't help, we no longer bend our knee." (Hegel Works, Vol. 13, p. 142).

As a media theorist *avant la lettre*, it is also Hegel's discovery that the progressive development of knowledge affects the medium of optimal representation of knowledge. As art has not stood still in its development, the associated topos of the end of art accompanies its further development in almost two centuries since Hegel in such a way that the reason for this is adjusted with the respective development of the rationalization of the world. Thus, *Walter Benjamin* argues with his considerations on the reproducibility of works of art in the 1930s a thesis of the end of visual art in the transition from painting to the mass medium film. He attributes to film the potential to perform the enlightening work that the classical artwork cannot do due to its specific being as a medium bound to originality and aura and grown from ritual contexts. According to Benjamin, the painter still appears like an archaic magician compared to the cameraman, who with his new device can penetrate "deep into the tissue of the given" (Benjamin, 1935/2003, p. 32) in a very scientific and surgeon-like manner.

In the 1990s, it is then Arthur Danto who argues that modern art has in a way stopped wanting to be art. According to his analysis, it marks a transition to a takeover of art by philosophy, because it confronts the recipient primarily with philosophical questions. The discovery about the end made by the *conceptual art* that began with Duchamp is therefore that art is no longer art, but philosophy: "(…) it little matters whether art is philosophy in action or philosophy is art in thought." (Danto, 1986, p. 113).

These further developments of Hegel's analysis also make it clear that the end of art is not to be equated with its disappearance. Despite technological progress and the discoveries of the avant-garde, it is also not the case that the effect of art has completely migrated from the emotions to the intellect. Certainly, we do not fall on our knees in silent devotion before certain emotionally gripping modern paintings, such as a triptych by *Francis Bacon,*. However, art does take place within a wide playing field that includes both hyper-rational and emotionally affective elements, which, as *Arnold Gehlen* emphasizes, provide *relief* from the conformist demands of the rationalized modern world (cf. Gehlen, 1960/1986, p. 222). We may therefore assume that art will continue to develop and perfect itself within its domain even after the transition to secular societies shaped by mass media, and that it will continue to explore the limits of its possibilities with increasing precision.

The media background noise against which this development in art is taking place today is very different from all previous art epochs due to the development of digital media. Even though the term *Metaverse* has been used exclusively for future ubiquitous interfaces that mimic three-dimensional spatiality based on the Internet for some time now, this designation seems appropriate for the already existing metasphere of information that has spread over the world with the Internet. Books, newspapers, magazines, cinema films, and television still exist, but in the mass medium of the

Internet, the dissolution of the aura described by Walter Benjamin reaches a completely different level. Certainly, emotionally gripping and increasingly immersive experiences can be made in these digital worlds. However, content propagates so quickly and uncontrollably on everyone's digital device that there seems to be no room left for aura-charged, original works.

Looking at NFTs, the main question is initially not about regaining an emotionally charged aura. Rather, this technology provides a rational answer to the question of determining originality in the sense of identity in the digital space. From the perspective of the computer scientist, it appears as a problem to be solved to treat originality itself as information that can be conveyed in the digital medium. As with the reference to a specific point on a star map, it is about determining that the image stored at a specific location in the network is the original. The technology that solves this problem is the blockchain, which is a digital certificate that has information about a digital object to be distinguished from it. Specifically, this certificate is a chain of encrypted information units, so-called *blocks,* which are stored in multiple copies in a decentralized *peer-to-peer network*. With every action that relates to the digital asset associated with it, cryptographically encrypted information about this action is added to the chain. Through a system of regularly occurring authentication of blocks to specific information on the chain by the decentralized network, it is protected from the insertion of illegitimate information blocks. It is also a matter of information processing in the blockchain whether the digital objects stored on it are exchangeable and in principle divisible, *fungible tokens* or those that always remain as a whole and are thus *non-fungible tokens* (NFTs).

Thus, the same blockchain can contain information about both the tokens of a crypto currency that can be broken down into smaller units and indivisibleindividual tokens. In their interplay with each other, we may then have to do with digital art traded in the fungible crypto currency *Ethereum* on the online portal *Opensea* in connection with non-fungible tokens, NFTs. It is important that the blockchain does not protect against the copy of the digital image associated with it. The NFT does not guarantee the numerical uniqueness of a digital object, but only certifies that the image linked with it at a specific location on the Internet is the original. Regardless of this, the digital graphic associated with an NFT, like any other image on the Internet, can be copied without effort and infinitely reproduced in the same quality as the original.

Although the same image in the same quality can be stored on any digital device without any financial effort, the investments made mainly on Opensea in visual art in the form of NFTs reached a trading volume of approx. 17 billion US$ in 2021 (Nonfungible & L'Atelier, 2021, p. 34). However, a rapid crash set in at the beginning of 2022, which is still ongoing during the 2nd half of the year. The reasons for this up and down in the NFT economy are diverse. It is also not to be ruled out that the enthusiasm in 2021 coincides with the peak of this form of digital art and thus with the end of the development history of NFTs themselves. In that case, the process of trial and error associated with high financial investments would have already revealed the function of NFTs in a comprehensive sense.

To get closer to the meaning of this, it is revealing to compare a general idea of digital originals with those digital artworks that have achieved top prices. If we first turn to the general idea, it can be paraphrased that NFTs answer the question of confirming the originality of already existing artworks in the digital space. In one of the many relevant *YouTube videos*, for example, there is talk of the up-and-coming artist named *Susan* who is looking for protection for her online exhibition of digital painting. After Susan receives the necessary information from her friend Mark, she decides to have NFTs created for her artworks. The fact that she can sell her customers clearly certified originals through this technology contributes to a notable success of her exhibition. It is important to see that we are talking about two worlds here that initially have nothing to do with each other. Neither the nature nor the existence of the artworks has anything to do with the NFT technology itself. Rather, the assumption is that these works are created independently of the NFT technology, speak aesthetically for themselves, and the connection with a certificate on a blockchain is the technical answer to the question of originality in the handling of art sales (see Simplilearn, 2021).

Undoubtedly, this approach corresponds to the use of NFT technology in countless cases. On the other hand, it can also be argued that the NFTs traded for a lot of money were created in response to the new technical possibilities. The significance of the artworks of this digital avant-garde is thus highly dependent on this technology and the skillful handling of the new medium, and to a much lesser extent on the intrinsic aesthetic quality of what is depicted. A non-representative, but nevertheless indicative impression of this is provided by the five NFT providers with the highest sales volume for digital artifacts over seven days in July 2022. These are *CryptoPunks* and *Meebits* from *Larva Labs*, the art platform *Art Blocks*, the NFT project *Bored Ape Yachtclub* which is probably the best known outside the scene, and the proto-adventure project called *Loot* (cf. NonFungible.com, 2022).

The oldest provider in this list in the short history of NFTs are the *CryptoPunks*, which were developed by the founders of the software company *Larva Labs* and released as NFTs in a limited edition of 10,000 in June 2017 (cf. Klein, 2019). On 24*24 pixels each, they depict the heads of outsiders and eccentrics in the style of 8-bit graphics from the 1990s, which differ from each other in terms of the combination of certain characteristics. It should also be noted that CryptoPunks refer to technical discoveries in two ways. They not only use NFTs, but also the possibilities of generative AI, which was still in an early phase and is now easily accessible to everyone via platforms like *Midjourney, DALL-E* or *Stable Diffusion* . In 2017, however, this was still a technology in its infancy, which is why the authenticity of the *CryptoPunks* project can also be traced back to the non-repeatability of this early experimental phase. They also refer to the anarchist movement of the *Cypherpunks* in their creation (cf. Hughes, 1993). This reference underlines that it was not primarily about *art,* but about a project exploring the possibilities of artificial intelligence and property rights on the internet. This lack of explicit *artistic intent* does not speak against the later flourishing trade with CryptoPunks as digital art. Rather, the origin story can tie into the varied myth of the artist as an unexpected genius, as described in the studies of *Ernst Kris* and *Otto Kurz* on the *Legend of the Artist* (1934/1995). Where we are supposed to imagine the young *Giotto* as a drawing shepherd, whose talent shows unexpectedly (ibid., p. 29 ff.), the contemporary occupation of the software engineer corresponds to the idea of a person with talent and unclouded access to the material, who becomes an artist rather by chance.

It becomes more than clear not only based on the outstanding position of CryptoPunks in the rankings of the most expensive NFTs that Larva Labs has succeeded in building a strong brand for NFT with these "original NFTs" of the first generation, as described by the auction house Christies (2021). The strength of CryptoPunks is also evident from the NFT project *Meebits* launched by Larva Labs in May 2021, which is advertised with them. This project consists of 20,000 3D avatars, which were automatically created according to certain parameters and whose block aesthetics remind of figures from the digital world of Minecraft (cf. Matney, 2022). The special feature of Meebits, in addition to the graphically detailed execution, which also includes animation elements, is a proprietary fee-free marketplace that allows transactions in crypto currency as well as the exchange of Meebits among each other. Despite these additional possibilities and the much more elaborate graphics, Meebits appear far less original and their relative success compared to similar projects seems to be based largely on the strength of the parent brand Larva Labs and their CryptoPunks.

The platform *Art Blocks*, which opened in November 2020, is particularly tailored to the conditions of the blockchain and offers series of works by different artists. The work "Fidenza #631" (NonFungible.com, 2022), sold by the artist *Tyler Hobbs* on July 12, 2022 for approximately $500,000, shares two additional characteristics with all other artworks on this platform, in addition to its serial nature. Its genesis is only attributable to the artist insofar as he only sets the boundary conditions for the subsequent creation of the artworks in the computer language *Processing* according to certain algorithms. The buyer of the work can then select certain additional parameters, and the work is calculated randomly after the first purchase has been made. It is therefore also a matter of luck whether a work that is particularly successful in the eyes of the buyer and community is created, which plays a decisive role in terms of a high resale value compared to the other artifacts in the series (cf. Waters, 2022). The adaptation to the digital medium does not end here, but also refers to the medium of the works. Unlike most NFT artworks, which are based on a link between the digital object and the distinguishable blockchain, these are blocks of information that are stored directly as code on the blockchain at the moment of their creation (cf. Art Blocks, 2023). The certificate on the blockchain therefore not only refers to the specific location where the original is stored on the internet; it also contains the information for creating the digital work itself. Due to the limitation of storage possibilities on the blockchain, the aesthetics of these works are as tailored to the possibilities of the technology as they move within the limited possibilities of the programming language *Processing* used for this purpose. The interaction of these limitations results in a minimalist aesthetic that conveys an intellectual claim and artistic high quality, as we know it from Minimal Art since the 1960s.

The *Bored Ape Yacht Club* made perhaps the biggest media waves outside the NFT community with its release by *Yuga Labs* on April 30, 2021. The origin story launched by the founders of Yuga Labs links the project with imagined crypto-billionaires in ape form who, in 2031, hang around rich and bored in an "apocalyptic Tiki bar", the *Bored Ape Yacht Club* (cf. Chayka, 2021). The artworks are a collection of 10,000 illustrations of ape portraits, whose individual design results from the different combination of certain attributes of different frequency determined by an AI algorithm. The astronomical increase in value of the avatars, which were sold indiscriminately for about $200 in the issue, based on the rarity of combinations of certain attributes, appears like a commentary on the subject of the project, which emerged from the crypto scene idiom "to ape in" for a risky full investment in crypto currencies.

Not only in this origin narrative, which is very similar to the anarchistic tone of the CryptoPunks, is there an awareness of integrating the works into a larger narrative. The project is also designed for the lively continuation of an open narrative by the buyers of the works. Thus, the Bored Ape Yacht Club is not only a website aimed at marketing the NFTs, but also a club of Bored Apes NFT owners, which gives them access to private areas on the website—for example, a toilet area where they can immortalize themselves with a digital graffiti (cf. Erinfolami, 2022). Bored Apes also serve as tickets for exclusive offline events, where many prominent owners of rare specimens are expected. Finally, the story of the Bored Ape Yacht Club is continued in that the full usage rights for the respective character are associated with the purchase of an NFT. The brand equity of the Bored Apes Yacht Club associated with the acquired likeness can thus also be used for own commercial projects (cf. Ye, 2021).

This principle of the narrative shaped by the buyers of the NFTs themselves is finally radically intensified with the project *Loot* launched in August 2021. These NFTs consist of lists of equipment items, designed in white typography on a black background, that we have known since the beginnings of adventure games. Unlike *Dungeons and Dragons* and its descendants, however, Loot does not provide a specific world with specific adventures and rules. Rather, it is left to the community itself to decide what ideas it has about visual appearances and properties of the world in which the items can be used. More than the subjective continuation of the Bored Ape Yacht Club's narrative, the Loot project is thus designed for a fantasy world built on the ideas of the community. With this, the creators of the Loot project see themselves as an alternative to the top-down model of the traditional culture industry, which, like *Marvel Comics*, plans its universes from the top down in management offices using large financial resources. In contrast, this bottom-up model is about the community participating in the increase in value of the intellectual property it has created through its own further development of the project (cf. Russel, 2021). In its extreme form, this shows that in the world of NFTs, alongside the mainstream of quasi-realistic comic pop art, a more abstract language of form has developed. It is also noteworthy how much the NFTs of Loot not only externally resemble works by conceptual artists such as the artist *Lawrence Weiner* who works with concrete poetry, who long before this project followed the artistic strategy of shifting the actual work as far as possible into the world of the viewer's associations.

Even though the description of these five projects only scratches the surface of the iceberg, insights can be derived from them about digital artworks as NFTs that form the basis for predictions about their future. First of all, it should be noted that NFT art begins where Duchamp ends. His discovery that interchangeable objects can also be art is the rule in the digital medium. Just as Duchamp signs an interchangeable urinal and introduces it as an original into the world of art exhibitions, NFTs always identify a specimen linked to the blockchain from potentially infinite specimens as the original. In view of this, the advantage of serial works over individual works as NFTs becomes clear. Since the digital medium leaves no room for qualitative differences in the craftsmanship of drawing or painting, which could be used to identify the individuality of certain works, the randomness of an artificial intelligence algorithm and the associated *relative rarity* of certain automatically determined combinations within the series takes its place.

This rarity criterion, which is already important for the CryptoPunks, is responsible for the fact that the special graphic design is not unimportant, but as a quality feature it only needs to be of interest as far as it appears useful for differentiation within the series. Even if there is a tendency to attribute a high design quality to particularly rare works, the value of NFTs thus depends largely on mathematical parameters. The less likely certain combinations are, the higher the resale price that can be achieved for the respective NFT (cf. Perez, 2022). The monetary value of an object in the series then results almost mathematically from the popularity of the NFT project and the rarity of an individual object. It is therefore only logical that CryptoPunk #5822, one of the most expensive NFTs ever traded, represents a rarity within the series. Not only is it one of only 9 aliens in the series, but it is also one of only 481 portraits depicted with a bandana as headgear (cf. Diamond, 2022).

Establishing this leads to the decisive argument for a thesis of the *end of art* anticipated by NFTs. Where 20th century conceptual art marks the end of classical art by referring aesthetically arbitrary objects to philosophical questions, NFTs reach this limit by providing aesthetically arbitrary, immaterial artifacts answers to the question of the appreciation of art. The discovery made here about the end of art through the art production itself would therefore be that visual art is no longer art, but essentially a commercial product. In a variation of Danto's dictum, one could phrase it something like this: *"It little matters whether your money materializes in an artwork, or the art stays as immaterial as an entry in your checking account."*

As in the case of the classical avant-garde, the commentary accompanying the artworks is crucial for the acceptance of this shift. Thus, Duchamp's ordinary objects could only become important works of art because he—consciously and aggressively—introduced them into the art discourse at the same time (cf. Roche et al., 1917, p. 4 ff.). In contrast, NFTs, which mostly originated outside the official art discourse, rely on narratives and myth-making, as we know it from the construction of commercial brands. It certainly goes too far to speak of the end of the individual artist in this context. However, it is noticeable that the NFT narrative is less about artists and designers than about the collective of publishers and the names of the series. For example, the artist working under the pseudonym *Seneca*, who developed the template for the Bored Apes, is only peripherally associated with the success of the series (cf. Khanna, 2021). Bearing this in mind, the discovery made with the development of NFTs can be described as the digital artwork being meaningful not as a single original, but as a serial product of a brand curated by a creative team. We are still largely dealing with artifacts from a founding phase in which the myth is still writing itself. Seen in this way, CryptoPunks are the *Levi's Jeans* among the NFTs, whose success largely depends on the image and the associated narratives of being the first product of its kind. The strong brand here arises from the thing itself. In contrast, not only the significantly less successful Meebits, but especially the many other completely unknown projects with similar strategies, show that this success cannot simply be repeated. The necessity of embedding later generation NFTs into a well-considered and strategically deployed narrative becomes clear with the *Bored Ape Yachtclub*, which is not a project of the first hour, but one of the first to approach the medium with a sophisticated branding and marketing strategy.

All of this does not necessarily speak against the aesthetic quality of the works or their existence as meaningful works of art. In particular, projects by Art Blocks and Loot point in this direction. Similarly, the assumption that NFTs lead to an actual auratic charging of the JPG image in one's own digital wallet cannot be refuted with reference to material insubstantiality, interchangeability, or commercial interest, any more than the emotional significance of one's own star for the protagonist mentioned at the beginning. Both ultimately lie in the eye and feeling of the respective viewer.

It is difficult to predict whether the market for NFTs will take off again in the future as it has in the past. Much suggests a hype that will not repeat itself in the same way. Nevertheless, NFT art sheds light on previous art. Just as Duchamp's Readymade, the extreme case, clarifies the artist's power of positioning, which is also contained in all works of art, the extreme case of NFT art highlights the always included share of market and brand in them. Thus, one can already take the stylistic recognizability in various works of art by an artist, his signet, and the mythical transfiguration of artist biographies as prototypical for branding beyond the art world.

The engagement with, for example, *Da Vinci, van Gogh, Picasso* or *Warhol*, whose works and style are recognized everywhere in the world, can lead to the assumption that artworks can also be assigned to a *brand*. In addition, with regard to NFTs, it can be noted that artworks can be designed as brands that, in their own way, meet the need for originality, aura, and emotional *relief* in the midst of a rationalized world.

References

Art Blocks. (2023). How it works. https://www.artblocks.io/info/how-it-works. Accessed 20 Dec. 2023.
Benjamin, W. (2003). *Das Kunstwerk im Zeitalter seiner technischen Reproduzierbarkeit.* Edition Suhrkamp (Originalwerk veröffentlicht 1935).
Klein, J. (23 January 2019). How CryptoPunks' Creators Charmed the Art World and Paved the Way for Blockchain Art. https://web.archive.org/web/20210409025146/https://breakermag.com/how-cryptopunks-creators-charmed-the-art-world-and-paved-the-way-for-blockchain-art/. Accessed 10 Jan. 2024.
Chayka, K. (30 July 2021). Why bored ape avatars are taking over twitter. The New Yorker. https://www.newyorker.com/culture/infinite-scroll/why-bored-ape-avatars-are-taking-over-twitter. Accessed 9 Aug. 2022.
Christie's. (8 April 2021). 10 Things to Know About CryptoPunks, the Original NFTs. https://www.christies.com/features/10-things-to-know-about-Crypto-Punks-11569-1.aspx. Accessed 10 Jan. 2024.
Danto, A. (1986). *The Philosophical Disenfranchisement of Art.* Columbia University Press.
Diamond, A. (21 February 2022). $24 Million! Secret Behind the Highest Ever CryptoPunk #5822. https://medium.com/nswap/24-million-secret-behind-the-highest-ever-cryptopunk-5822-f3ee997e48e9. Accessed 14 Dec. 2023.
Erinfolami, K. (6 April 2022) Bored Ape Yacht Club: What Is It & Why Are They So Expensive? https://www.makeuseof.com/what-is-bored-ape-yacht-club/. Accessed 10 Jan. 2024.
Fukuyama, F. (1992). The End of History and the Last Man. New York: Free Press.
Gehlen, A. (1986). *Zeit-Bilder. Zur Soziologie und Ästhetik der modernen Malerei* (3. erweiterte Aufl.). Klostermann (Originalwerk veröffentlicht 1960).
Hegel, G. W. F. (1986). *Werke in 20 Bänden, Bd. 13* (1st edn.). Vorlesungen über die Ästhetik I.
Hughes, E. (1993). A Cypherpunk's Manifesto. https://www.activism.net/cypherpunk/manifesto.html. Accessed 15 July 2022.
Jaeschke, W. (2010). *Hegel-Handbuch: Leben – Werk – Schule.* Verlag J. B. Metzler.

Khanna, M. (31 January 2021). Meet the Woman Artist Who Made the Insanely Popular 'Bored Ape' NFT Logo. https://www.indiatimes.com/technology/news/woman-artist-bored-ape-nft-seneca-560808.html. Accessed 10 Jan. 2024.

Kris, E., & Kurz, O. (1934/1995). *Die Legende vom Künstler: Ein geschichtlicher Versuch.* Suhrkamp.

Nonfungible & L'Atelier. (Hrsg.). (2021). Yearly NFT market Report 2021. https://nonfungible.com/reports/2021/en/yearly-nft-market-report. Accessed 13 May 2023.

Liu, C. (2019). *Jenseits der Zeit: Roman.* Deutsche Erstausgabe. Wilhelm Heyne.

Matney, L. (4 May 2022). CryptoPunks Maker Larva Labs Launches Their New NFT Project, Meebits.https://techcrunch.com/2021/05/03/CryptoPunks-maker-larva-labs-launches-their-new-nft-project-meebits/.

NonFungible. (2022). Market Tracker. Highest 7 days sales. https://nonfungible.com. Accessed 15 July 2022.

Perez, M. (4 February 2022). Top 10 Most Expensive CryptoPunks Ever Sold. https://www.parsehub.com/blog/most-expensive-CryptoPunks/. Accessed 20 Dec. 2023.

Roche, H.-P., Wood, B., & Duchamp, M. (Eds.). (1917). *The Blind Man, No. 2. New York (facsimile).* http://sdrc.lib.uiowa.edu/dada/blindman/index.htm. Accessed 13 May 2023.

Russel, K. (3 September 2021). The Loot Project Flips the Script on NFTs – TechCrunch. https://techcrunch.com/2021/09/03/loot-games-the-cryptoworld/. Accessed 20 Dec. 2023.

Simplilearn. (2021). NFT explained in 5 minutes. https://www.youtube.com/watch?v=NNQLJcJEzv0. Accessed 20 Dec. 2023.

Waters, K. (8 May 2022). Art Blocks and the Data of Generative Art. https://www.rightclicksave.com/article/art-blocks-and-the-data-of-generative-art. Accessed 20 Dec. 2023.

Ye, J. (5 December 2021). NFT in Hong Kong: Bored Ape Yacht Club Owners Seek Merchandise Deals, Art Exhibitions for Cartoon Primates. https://www.scmp.com/tech/tech-trends/article/3158391/nft-hong-kong-bored-ape-yacht-club-owners-seek-merchandise-deals. Accessed 23 Dec. 2023.

Afterword

The Stay-Puft Marshmallow Man! He was on all the packages we used to buy when I was a kid. We used to roast Stay-Puft marshmallows at Camp Waconda!
Ray Stantz, played by Dan Aykroyd

The scene from *Ivan Reitman's* Ghostbusters (1984), in which the fictional brand mascot *Stay-Puft Marshmallow Man* turns out to be the final boss in the fight against evil, not only evokes a feeling of nostalgic longing in many people over forty. For both, the character *Ray Stantz*, who can't imagine anything more innocent than an advertising figure from his own childhood, and those who associate their youth in the 1980s with the iconic logo of the real brand *Ghostbusters*, this scene exemplifies how deeply brand myths are rooted in our culture. From this, one can visualize the plethora of brands whose myths are intertwined with one's own biography.

As an objection to this insight underlying the analyses presented here into the relevance of *brand and myth*, one could argue that the perspective is distorted. If you have only a hammer as a tool, you see every problem as a nail; and if you view the world of brands solely through the prism of myth, you will find it everywhere. With this in mind, it is important to emphasize that such blinkers have been consciously put on for analytical purposes, with the constant awareness that they can be taken off at any time. Even if it resonates more or less explicitly in the individual texts, let it be said clearly here once again: The considerations do not question that brands stand for products whose benefits, understood in the broadest sense, are crucial for their success. If this constellation is not given for a brand, no one will warm up to its myth for even a Kodak moment.

On the other hand, anyone who speaks of a strong brand and means only the emotional bond through emotional storytelling and striking visual communication loses sight of this context. Therefore, one should not fall into the fallacy that a media-fabricated myth alone is sufficient to give a brand (new) strength. But also the opposite idea, that a brand can do without myth, does not do justice to its concept. One would then assume that brands are nothing more than interchangeable names and graphic elements on products. If they then no longer stood for any narrative that goes beyond the boundaries of the immediate, we could understand them as signs, but no longer in their meaning as symbols. For a full understanding of brands, on the other hand, it should be noted that they are just as dependent on myth as myth itself cannot be maintained without points of reference in the world outside its own narrative.

If we follow this thought, it becomes clear once again that we can only understand brands in interaction with a world in which their myths have just as much impact as they depend on it. Brands thus transcend the relationship between buyer and product and gain cultural relevance even beyond their own target group. The analysis of brands therefore contributes to an understanding of culture that goes beyond them. I hope that with this book I have made a contribution to the discussion and stimulated deeper reflection on the subtle ways in which brands and their personalities shape our culture.

A strong brand, that is such a personality in *one* case.

Ningbo
in January 2024

Stefan Waller

GPSR Compliance

The European Union's (EU) General Product Safety Regulation (GPSR) is a set of rules that requires consumer products to be safe and our obligations to ensure this.

If you have any concerns about our products, you can contact us on

ProductSafety@springernature.com

In case Publisher is established outside the EU, the EU authorized representative is:

Springer Nature Customer Service Center GmbH
Europaplatz 3
69115 Heidelberg, Germany